MORALITY, ANYONE?

MORALITY, ANYONE?

WILLIAM LESTER, S.J.

ARLINGTON HOUSE • PUBLISHERS
NEW ROCHELLE, NEW YORK

Library of Congress Catalog Card Number 74-30133

ISBN 0-87000- 297-x

Manufactured in the United States of America

Library of Congress Cataloging in Publication Data

Lester, William, 1921-
    Morality anyone?

    A collection of the author's articles which appeared
in 1973 in his newspaper column, The moral angle.
    Includes index.
    1. Ethics. 2. Social ethics. I. Title.
BJ1031.L47   170   74-30133
ISBN 0-87000-297-X

To my little sister,
Mary,
who started all of this.

Contents

MORALITY, ANYONE?

Introduction

I remember while a theological student years ago the moral professors stating that under ordinary circumstances the United States citizen who cheats on his income tax is not bound to restitution because of the probability of the tax system being unjust. To my disconcertment they did not elaborate and say why the taxes were probably unjust. Mystifying, too, was the fact that they weren't speaking out to the general public who had the practical stake in the issue; rather they were speaking only to quite disinterested, non-tax-paying seminarians. But at least they were tackling a problem almost unique for them in its up-to-the-minute practicality. Usually they stuck to standard issues from dusty, old tomes and let the world grope and stumble on its own through the difficulties of the day involving their area of expertise—the human fittingness of things.

Later, for a group of laymen who wanted answers to practical, moral questions and were willing to pay well for them I sought answers, by telephone, from the philosophical and theological departments of eight or nine major universities in North America laying claim to some excellence in those faculties. I got nowhere. One man with a large family to feed was anxious to write a short treatise on the morality of prizefighting, a subject of his own choosing; but the outline I gave him suggesting the type of logical treatment the sponsors expected put him so much in awe of my analytical power that I was sure that he wouldn't do. And he didn't. Another man, a dean of a law school, wrote a good paper but one far beyond the comprehension of the ordinary layman. He had to go. Another person assured me that no one in his entire graduate school was treating anything as practical as the morality of prizefighting, taxes, privacy, and so forth. He himself wrote his doctorate on the "evolution of the philosophical thought of the sixteenth century French peasant."

Consequently, when my sister one day suggested that I write a newspaper column fielding current moral questions I was quite aware of the need and of the lack of anyone filling the need. Sure enough, the column, *The Moral Angle*, using a question and answer format caught on quickly and during the last ten years has steadily gained momentum. It is now syndicated nationally by Copley News Service in an estimated seventy-five papers.

This present book is a collection of the best items appearing in the column during 1973.

The book, I should warn you, is not the type to be read through at one sitting. There simply is too much philosophical thought to be weighed. Probably a chapter is all that could be taken at a sitting and still have the arguments appreciated. After all, the book says in a hundred or two hundred words what the usual, intellectual talk-show on television would take an hour to say. Yet it's the type of book which you may want to keep for reference, for a third and fourth look at this answer or that.

Hopefully my work will be interesting to you who think for yourselves and do not accept on blind faith conclusions from opinion makers; to you who want scientific progress channeled in a human direction so that it will not dehumanize while it provides more food, better entertainment, cleaner environment or whatever; to you in medicine, law, politics, news media, economics, love and marriage who want guidelines in your respective fields to keep you on the human path.

From experience I know of two general obstacles to appreciating my work: departmentalization of education and the latter's rather complete disregard today for philosophy. The man with his doctor of medicine degree tends to think that he, not the philosopher, defines life and death and determines in the abstract when death takes place and that he, not the moralist, has the determining word on the morality of euthanasia, abortion, and so on. The same can be said for the newsman. He tends to think that because his whole life is spent in journalism, he also has all the moral answers, say, about his profession's right of secrecy. And so it is with people in other walks of life. Often, though, the same people who don't recognize the place of a moralist in their life speciality will welcome the solutions of moralists in other people's.

Those of you who will enjoy this work owe a thanks to my sister, Mary Lester, for initiating the original project and to her and Rose Ann Anderson and Jesuits Richard A. Hill, John F. Dullea, Donald J. Duggan for their intelligent, kind, patient criticisms. I certainly am in their debt.

Chapter 1
Old and New Morality

Q

Is there a radical difference between the old and "new" morality?

What is the "New Morality" and how does it differ from the old?

A

"New Morality," otherwise known as situation ethics, denies absolute standards of morality and declares that circumstances alone matter. It is philosophical relativism, which contradictorily proposes as an absolute truth that there is no absolute truth, applied to morality. It leads inevitably to the pernicious doctrine that a good end justifies immoral means; that robbery and murder, for example, are permissible when the stakes to be won appear in the doer's judgment heavier in benefits towards mankind than the crimes in harm. Of course, it gives no end of encouragement to revolution-terrorists.

Along with the relativism largely dominating law, art,

philosophy, economics, theology, political and social sciences the New Morality is responsible for the permissiveness sweeping the world.

The old morality on which our Western civilization was founded affirms that man has a definite, objective way of acting in order to fulfill himself as man, like a clock has in order to fulfill itself as a clock. Reason uncovers, for the most part, this norm for correct human living by first uncovering the nature of man and then learning from the nature what is required to perfect it. Reason sees, for instance, that such actions as murder, robbery, lies and slander are opposed to the very nature of man and that, since there is no greater good for man than his fulfillment as a human, he must suffer the collapse of the entire universe rather than lessen his intrinsic worth by murdering, robbing, etc.

As far as circumstances are concerned, traditional morality understands them as determining, say, whether a killing was justifiable or unjustifiable, accidental or intentional, and, if unjustifiable, the extent of guilt; but it never understands them as changing an intentional, direct killing of an innocent person into a morally good act.

Q

Do Humanists follow the old or "new" morality?

Leaders within the Humanist movement met in New York recently and signed a document called Humanist Manifesto II. (Philosopher John Dewey was a signer of Humanist Manifesto I in 1933.) I would like your critique of the following statements about ethics in the document:

"We affirm that moral values derive their source from human experience. Ethics is autonomous and situational, needing no ideological sanctions. Ethics stems from human need and interest. To deny this distorts the whole basis of life."

A

Contrary to the Humanists, moral values have their source not in experience—the way a golfer sometimes discovers a better swing—but in the very nature of man. For example: because man is by nature a social-animal, he needs the association of his fellow men in order to develop fully as a human; thus, any action on his part, like stealing and lying, which naturally destroys that association, blocks his development and is immoral. Human experience alone could never lead to such an absolute statement against stealing and lying; it could come only to a general probability with lots of room for exceptions to be made by the clever and determined.

The next statement of the Humanists unequivocally declares for situation ethics, otherwise known as the "new" morality.

The final two statements, except possibly for the word "interest," can be used by both the old and "new" morality. The difference, though, lies in the basis for man's needs. Traditional morality sees it as man's nature; the "new" morality as the situation in which man finds himself.

For the Humanists, life will always be complex. They never will be able to know with certainty how to be happy.

Chapter 2

Science and Human

Life Engineering

Q

Is cloning—the asexual means of reproduction—permissible?

Would it be moral to bring a person into the world through cloning?

Cloning is an asexual means of reproduction. It's worked successfully with frogs and theoretically would work equally well with humans. In it scientists replace the nucleus of the ovum with a nucleus of a cell taken perhaps from the skin of the mother or someone else. The ovum is then put back. The offspring that's born is an identical copy of whoever provided the nucleus. So the whole world could be populated with carbon copies of Richard Nixon.

A

Man does not have absolute dominion over human life. He has only a certain stewardship over it. He cooperates in beginning new life and cares for it once it has arrived. He is not lord and master who may order up new life, treat it in whatever way he thinks best, and end it whenever it suits his purpose. God alone has that direct dominion. He created man for Himself and ordinarily expresses through nature His will about human life.

It is obvious that nature has appointed sexual intercourse as the one and only means for summoning new human life into existence. Consequently, married couples have a right to the act and may aid nature, if necessary, in her process of human generation; but they may not supplant her with cloning or even artificial insemination.

Moreover, cloning a child would deprive him of his natural right to two parents since it would leave him with blood ties to only one. The deprivation would be immoral.

Perhaps it should be noted, too, that fertilization of a human ovum cannot produce of itself an intellectual soul which makes the individual a person. The intellectual soul is immaterial and can only be created by God. But it could be questioned whether God would cooperate in the usurpation of His dominion to the extent of giving the cloned being an intellectual soul. Without that soul the being would be merely a humanoid having the physical appearances of a human but the animating principle only of an animal.

Nations holding for the sacredness of human life ought to outlaw cloning as an act against that principle, the breaching of which cannot but be destructive of the community.

Q

What is the moral angle to the deep freeze used by the Cryonic Society?

Not long ago an 8-year-old girl died of a kidney problem. Her father had a Cryonic Society cool her body to 327 degrees below zero and store it in liquid nitrogen so that some time in the future when medical science may know how

to cure the particular kidney ailment, the girl possibly could
be brought back to life and made healthy again.
  What's the morality of this deep freeze?

A

The hope of the Cryonic Society seems unreasonable; hence the time, money and resources spent on freezing the dead appear an immoral waste.

When the body is so indisposed that the intellectual soul can no longer use it, the union of body and soul ceases and the soul goes off to a life of its own. The soul, as the first principle of life, is made for activity. To remain in a completely useless body would be—like having its presence in a block of wood—against the very purpose of its existence. Therefore, as soon as the complete indisposition of the body has been finalized by nature, the soul leaves and is never to be brought back again by any amount of science.

If nature has not already sounded the toll before the Cryonic Society applies its deep freeze treatment, the treatment should surely do it.

Q

May parents pre-select the sex of their children?

Scientists are working with some success on separating the X and Y chromosomes in male animal sperm. The X bearing sperm produces females, the Y produces males. Sex pre-selection will mean millions of dollars for people with livestock.

Scientists are also working towards sex pre-selection for humans. What's the morality there?

A

As you seem to realize, there is no moral problem with sex pre-selection for animals. For humans, though, there is.

Humans may pre-select the sex of their child only on the provision that they do nothing to frustrate the natural process of generation. If wishing could select the sex of the coming child, parents would be free to wish.

Dominion over human life—including generation of life—belongs to God. Man can aid nature in generation, supply for deficiencies and so forth; but he is not morally free to thwart nature—or alter her, say, by adding a third arm and leg to children through genetic engineering.

But a scientific procedure which would kill either the X or Y chromosome in human sperm so there could be sex preselection would be thwarting the natural generation process. Furthermore, if killing one type of chromosome could be allowed, killing the other at the same time would also have to be allowed; yet killing both would result in contraception which is an obvious thwarting of nature and unjustifiable.

Q

Morally, may science control our emotions completely?

I've read various articles in recent periodicals and newspapers where some scientists believe that by the year 2,000 A.D. man can be completely controlled: he will have no deep feelings such as hate, lust, love, anger.

If this comes to pass and we are like robots, how can there be any moral angle involved?

A

The person who through no fault of his own cannot think and will as a responsible human does not merit or demerit morally. He is not free, though, to consent willfully to any reduction in his human responsibility; nor is anyone free to force him into such a reduction.

Man has a natural duty to seek his perfection. Love of good is the driving force to that goal; hatred of evil is the necessary reverse of the drive; anger gives the drive the needed force to overcome obstacles; indeed, all emotions have their part in leading him to perfection. No one else can fulfill man's duty for him, and everyone must respect his right to fulfill it. Hence, no one may take control of his emotions away from him; he needs them for his perfection. Depriving him of them would be tantamount to committing him to a living death.

Q

Will genetic intervention make us more moral?

Famous underwater explorer Jacques-Yves Cousteau stated that the evolutionary process of man will be speeded up by genetic intervention and the elimination of natural selection, and consequently man will soon be the immortal god-like master of the universe. Does that mean that evolution will make us more moral?

A

Evolution can directly affect the body only. It can have merely an indirect effect on the immaterial faculties of intellect and will through the change that it would bring about in the disposition of the body. But no bodily change can alter the nature of either immaterial faculty and thereby deprive, say, the will of its fundamental freedom. A material thing cannot act upon an immaterial thing. Thus, evolution or no evolution, man in this life cannot but always remain subject to the spiritual struggle involved in choosing good and rejecting evil. God, on the other hand, has no struggle; He can choose nothing but good.

Because evolution would equip man for greater intelligence through the refinement of his external and interior senses which gather the raw material for his intellect and because that added capability also means basically a greater potential for discerning good and evil, man would acquire at the same time a greater moral responsibility. But the greater responsibility simply would mean that he was being held accountable for more, deserving of a greater reward or punishment. Only responsibility fulfilled improves his moral status.

Q

Is it permissible to start and grow a baby in a test tube?

Scientists have reported the fertilization in test tubes of the human egg and the laboratory culture of the embryo. But Dr. Leon Kass, physician and biochemist at the National Academy of Sciences, was reported as fearing that the manipulation in the laboratory of the embryo could produce great damages to the future child because the processes have not been tested, and as questioning the morality of parents' right to have children "by methods which carry for that child an unknown and untested risk of deformity or malformation."

Is the doctor correct?

A

As far as the doctor went in his moral thinking, he is correct. Parents are not free to risk without a justifiable reason a deformity or malformation in their children. Scientific experimentation or parental convenience is no justifying reason. But there is much more wrong with the experiment than that.

First, human life belongs to God, not to scientists, parents or anyone else. Hence scientists are not free to experiment with human life, beginning and ending it as though it were nothing more than animal life. They are free only to assist human life, to preserve and improve it.

Second, a married couple's right to bring into existence a new life extends only to the use of the marital act which unites them as one principle of procreation. They are not free any more than the scientists to usurp God's dominion over life. They have no moral right, therefore, to participate in creating new life through a laboratory procedure. They may use the laboratory only to help nature preserve a life which otherwise would be endangered.

Third, a child who is conceived and brought to "birth" in a laboratory bottle would be deprived of a basis for necessary parental love, which natural conception, maturation in the womb, and birth provide. Without a justifying reason, he may not be deprived of that which he has a natural right to.

Q

May a person undergo a sex-change operation?

What's the morality of the sex-change operations being done at the Stanford Medical Center? Mostly homosexuals and lesbians, unhappy with their sex, come in for the gender change.

A

Apparently the purpose of the operation is to make the patient's acts of homosexuality more gratifyingly real or to allow the patient to assume more realistically the immoral role of transvestite. It is not to aid nature by correcting an abnormality. (People who have the operation still remain the male or female they were before the operation. Only some visual equipment of gender has been changed.)

For the patient, the operation is immoral. For the hospital, it amounts to formal cooperation in evil and is therefore immoral and must not be accepted as legitimate medical practice.

Q

Is psychosurgery moral?

Is it ever moral to use psychosurgery on people? A tiny portion of brain tissue can be excised by surgery, electricity, radiation or ultrasound and can make a violent tempered man placid. It's being done, but it has brought up a lot of controversy.

A

Psychosurgery which would merely excise an illness and leave no disproportionately harmful side effects such as a lessening of the patient's ability to be responsible for his actions is moral.

Psychosurgery which would turn the patient permanently into little more than a placidly emotional vegetable no longer responsible for his actions is moral when it is used to subdue the otherwise uncontrollable, dangerous violence of the incurably insane. It would also be moral as punishment in place of the death penalty. In neither case is the patient being deprived unjustly of his ability to direct his own response to life situations. And that same provision would have to be met in any other case.

Q

May brain surgery be used on violent prisoners?

Is it morally permissible for prisons to use brain surgery to turn violent inmates into more docile persons? The idea is to use neurosurgery to locate centers in the brain which may have been previously damaged and be causing violent behaviour.

A

To attribute all violent behaviour to brain damage is a mistake for it denies free will. To operate on that false assumption would harm unjustly those who freely willed their behaviour—unless the surgery could somehow be justified as punishment. (The criminal would have to be worthy of a punishment akin to death if his irascible power is destroyed or so diminished that he becomes imbecilicly helpless.)

To use surgery in order to explore for possible brain damage which may be causing violent behaviour seems permissible when (1) the harm to be avoided is worth the harm which the surgery will inflict, (2) there is not a less harmful way of achieving the same goal, (3) the prisoner-patient consents— unless the surgery can be justified as punishment. The same, likewise, can be said in the case of known brain damage causing the bad behaviour.

Q

May a woman have an ovary-transplant?

A woman in Argentina has had an ovary transplant. She's pregnant now and should give birth soon. The child will have the genetic traits of the woman who donated the ovaries. Doesn't that mean that the child is the donor's and not the woman's who will give birth to him? What's the morality of the whole thing?

A

Seemingly, conception and birth through an ovary transplant is nothing more than a radical implantation of a donor egg which is then fertilized by the recipient's husband. Such a method of conception is not morally permissible.

Generation of human life must be in accord with nature. By nature husband and wife have exclusive, inalienable rights over each other's body. Neither has a right to procreate except in full partnership with the other.

By nature, too, the child is the fruit of the union between husband and wife and consequently shares in the genetic traits of both.

Chapter 3
Money and Labor

Q

Must we work for work's sake, like the work ethic says?

There's been a lot of talk about the work ethic and working for work's sake. Is it true that labor is good in itself and that is why we consider laziness to be immoral?

A

Work is merely a means to an end. Most of us have to work, sometimes burdensomely, to earn our living. Even when bulging with money, we still have to work continually at our self-development as humans, which includes being productive members of the community. In any case, we work to attain a goal and to enjoy it. Happiness, not work, leads us on.

Working at self-development is, in a sense, more important than earning a living; yet we must first stay alive before we can work at self-development. As far as possible, though, even livelihood work ought to dovetail with self-development. Machines, schedules, allocations should be used to free us from backbreaking, boring tasks and for work requiring human, creative ingenuity.

Laziness is only immoral when it takes us from tasks of obligation.

Q

Ought steelworkers to have made a contract as they did which bound them to arbitration in all disputes?

The United Steelworkers Union and the companies agreed to settle their differences through binding arbitration. They say the agreement will work for the benefit of the employees, the companies, the customers and the nation. Both the union and companies will have equal bargaining leverage without interrupting the earnings of employees or the operations of the companies. The continual operation would cut down on U. S. imports and put more people to work here at home.

Isn't a contract like that with binding arbitration what you've been calling for?

A

Indeed. Congratulations to the Union and the companies for taking the step.

Their pact is hopefully the wave of the future. The present financial pinch has made the need for labor-management cooperation and the immaturity of settling differences through strikes and lockouts more and more obvious. Management, labor and the public sink or swim together.

Q

May public employees strike?

Should public employees have the right to strike? In one sense I think the public employees should have the same right as any other worker. But in another sense, having the police and firemen out on strike could be disastrous for the public.

A

Strikes are a type of warfare. But just as wars must not be allowed when there is a higher authority able to impose a peaceful, just settlement so strikes ought not to be allowed. If the battling parties cannot settle their differences peacefully on their own, then binding arbitration must be imposed on them.

The need for imposed settlement is especially evident in the case of public employees.

Q

Do strikers have a right to physically prevent others from working?

I don't contest the right of individual workers to leave their jobs when they are not satisfied with the terms of employment. But do they, when organized as a union, have the right to physically prevent others from working?

A

A civilized community should not allow parties in a dispute within her borders to settle their quarrel through force.

The community's duty is to see that justice prevails, and justice can be on the side of the weak as well as the strong. Remember the old adage, might does not make right.

When the community is not sufficiently organized to impose a settlement through impartial arbitration, the disputants are bound by the moral principles governing war.

Q

Did truckers have a right to block highways to demonstrate their grievances in the energy crisis?

What right did truckers have to block highways to make their point that they didn't like the 55 mile-per-hour speed limit and the rise in diesel fuel cost? Traffic was backed up for miles here in New Jersey.

A

Ordinarily demonstrations must be in accordance with law. Law co-ordinates everyone's rights and keeps the community running smoothly. Action contrary to law violates someone's rights and disrupts to some degree community life.

The truckers had a right to their unlawful demonstrations provided the following conditions, similar to those governing a just war, were met.

1) Lawful, harmless means of attaining the correction of injustice were not available.

2) The good to be achieved by the correction of the injustice outweighed the harm that the unlawful action would cause.

The reckoning of harm had to include that which might be done to others, say, to travelers with perhaps even life and death reasons for traveling uninterruptedly or to businessmen depending on delivery of perishable goods, that which might be done to the community by the example of disobedience to law, and that which might be caused by persons angered into taking the law into their own hands and retaliating against the truckers. Also, the weighing of good against evil had to take into consideration the certainty of each. A good with only a slim chance of being achieved normally does not justify causing with certainty an evil anywhere near comparable.

Personally, I thought the truckers were short on justice.

Q

May a union deny William F. Buckley, Jr. the right to speak on television unless he joins the union?

William F. Buckley, Jr., has a weekly television show. The American Federation of Television and Radio Artists demanded as a condition for his continuing that he join the union. He did so under protest and almost immediately brought a civil suit, charging that the union had no right to be in a position to deny him the right to speak freely over television.

I'm for both unions and free speech, and caught in the middle. Any answer?

A

A union should not be in a position to tyrannize over either its members or the employer. Its true position is that of a servant to the members, a partner to the employer, and a necessary instrument for the economic well-being of the community. Unfortunately it is not structured properly today and is therefore relatively free to tyrannize. And under that situation the worker, in my judgment, should be able to work without being forced to join a union. The fact, too, that he is free to join or not join would help to keep the union honest.

In the ideal economic order unions, management and the public would iron out their problems together. They would do so under the realization that they all sink or swim together, that what hurts one eventually hurts the others, that cooperation is the only profitable thing. Each would have his special sphere of interest. The public member of the triumvirate, in looking after the good of the community as a whole, would protect natural and civil rights so that someone like Buckley could speak out without having to get a paternalistic nod from his union.

Q

Is profit sharing in line with morality?

An ever increasing number of business companies in the United States are turning to profit sharing with employees. They find it a great way to increase production and lower costs.
What's the moral angle on profit sharing?

A

Profit sharing is a good step towards a morally ideal condition between management and labor.

By nature, labor and management are partners. Their job is to produce for the community and in producing to earn their own living. They are a team: each needs the other; to a great extent, what benefits one, benefits the other. The employee who is content and happy with his work is usually loyal, efficient, industrious and hence a moneymaker for the company; it behooves the company to make the employee happy with his work. In turn, the company that prospers secures the worker's employment. The partnership means that labor and management together are responsible for the company. Each has his own sphere of responsibility, yet neither rules autocratically. Together, for instance, somewhat like the guild system of old, they not only determine wages but also prices since the latter are so closely aligned with wages. Thus, profit sharing is a good step towards the team action that should exist between management and labor.

Unions as they are structured today have an intrinsic antagonism towards management and hence towards the partnership with management which is necessary for labor's complete fulfillment. Eventually organized labor must evolve away from such unions and into a better system. Unhappily, some labor bosses, selfishly determined to perpetuate their positions, will stand in the way. They are already trying to beat down profit sharing.

Q

How can absenteeism and sloppy work in a factory be avoided?

The factory worker in America gets good pay, yet he is often bored with the job—which makes for absenteeism and sloppy work. I'm trying to enhance employer-employee relations in my own plant and bring about job satisfaction. Any suggestions from a moral point of view?

A

Humanizing the employees' task as far as possible is a moral duty and at the same time an excellent business practice. It does not contribute to the "fast buck" but it helps assure the business a respected, long life.

The more a job resembles the work of a machine the more boring, monotonous, and stultifying it is. Besides deadening the man, it can have an adverse reaction on everyone he comes into contact with.

To be humanizing, jobs must have a creative aspect for only then can man find interest and satisfaction in his work.

The problem lies in forging a production system that allows for creativity and still meets the cost advantages of a dehumanizing assembly line. The task is not easy.

I am inclined to think that if the worker has to be given the choice between dehumanizing work or considerably less pay, he ought to choose the latter. He can be happy with fewer creature comforts. But sweating out eight unhappy hours every day, year in and year out, simply to relax a few hours—with job discontent still on his face—before a colored television set instead of a black and white one, or to drive to the shop in a large, powerful car instead of a small six-cylinder model, or to have a house with two and one-half baths instead of one is, in my judgment, not worth it.

Q

How would morality shape a national economy?

Do your moral principles say anything about the shape our economy should take? Our national financial situation seems to be floundering.

A

The basic principles governing any economic theory belong in the realm of morality. Morality determines the meaning of material resources in relation to man. The economist merely fleshes out the principles underlying this basic understanding. Should he build on an erroneous morality, his theory even though extremely sophisticated will be in disharmony with nature and must eventually crumble.

Two major economic principles of traditional morality tell us that (1) the world's material goods are meant for the use of everyone, (2) private ownership is necessary.

The first principle qualifies the dominion which ownership brings. It obliges the owner to consider his property as a type of public trust which he manages for the community's good. He is not free, for instance, to act on a pique and burn his factory down; he must consider the factory in relation to the needs of his employees and of the community in general.

A further corollary tells us that the employer and employee are partners, members of the same team producing for the good of the community. One manages but not without the say of the other since they work together as a team. Together, for example, they set prices and wages because both items are so intertwined; and they settle disputes not through strikes and lockouts but through binding arbitration so that production goes on smoothly and no one loses.

Also the principles seem to demand a controlled economy, one in which there can be a reasonable assurance of a wide, equitable distribution of the nation's material wealth. Control would start with labor-management-public councils at the lowest level, setting such things as production, prices and wages. Those determinations would be modified by representatives of the councils meeting in broader associations. Final adjustments would be made at the top by the broadest association which would be charged with supervising the economy of the entire nation. In this way controls would originate with the grassroots and not be imposed from above—as the Socialist countries do with disastrous results.

Q

Does an investor have a community responsibility?

Regents of the University of California turned down a proposal to consider the social responsibilities of a company before they invest in it. They ruled that their primary concern was to protect the financial investments of the University and that debating the social responsibilities of a company would open the doors intolerably to pressure groups and lobbyists.

How do you see it?

A

An investor may not use his money to promote or profit from evil. Thus the regents may not invest in gangsters even though the returns would be fabulous, nor in a company which they know is unjust to its employees.

An investor's efforts, however, must be primarily concerned with getting a good return on his money. That is his job. Much less effort can be spent on assurance that he is not unknowingly aiding a company that is robbing the public or its employees or polluting the atmosphere, etc. Ordinarily he is in no position to gather sufficient information for a reasonably sound judgment on such matters; investigating social injustices is not his line of work. He is obliged, though, to keep an interested eye and ear open and to clear up doubts that may come his way before he invests. Of course, the more money he intends to invest in a company the closer should be his scrutiny.

Q

Does the responsibility of charity-giving have limits?

By anyone's standards I have a considerable personal income. However, with fund drives sprouting up every single day and all seemingly worthy, even I could go broke by forever giving handouts.

What are my responsibilities according to traditional morality?

A

Generally 10% of a person's income is considered his responsibility to charity.

Through taxation the government usually collects that much and more for its various welfare and educational programs. So the amount due to charity is for the most part taken over by government action; anything the individual does on his own—donations to the church and other causes—ordinarily is beyond the call of duty.

In a sense it is unfortunate that government has taken over such a large part of the individual's charitable responsibilities. He recognizes that he pays for the government welfare programs where the people in need can get help, so he is inclined to feel free of personal obligation when someone in need approaches him. Let the person go to the government! Yet when he turns from personally helping the needy, he fails to exercise his generosity and, to a degree, has hardened his heart. Characterwise he loses and the loss affects the entire community.

Q

Should welfare recipients be allowed to organize and lobby?

You once said that welfare recipients should not be allowed to organize and lobby for more and more benefits. Would you explain that further?

A

The poor who are willing but unable to earn their living have a claim in social justice to be given the necessities of life from the abundance of others. They have a right to make known their needs and the duty of people to supply them when the needs are neglected. So a spontaneous demonstration by the poor, which requires some organization, could at times be necessary to spur people into a do-something attitude about correcting an injustice.

But an organization of welfare recipients that is set up to lobby on a permanent basis is another matter. The fact that it is continually lobbying implies ordinarily that the recipients already have the necessities and are now working on fringe benefits in an ever increasing amount. In other words, it implies that the welfarites have become "professional poor" and are using their organizing ability to usurp the property of others.

The very fact too that the welfare recipients have enough

money to support their organization is evidence that they are already receiving beyond their due in justice.

The standard of care for the poor ought to be determined by community administrators. It is to the community's advantage that she cares for the poor neither miserly nor with such a lavish hand that the "poor" become the envy of the average, productive citizen.

Q

Is money devaluation a form of stealing?

Recently the United States devalued the dollar. The people abroad who held billions of dollars suddenly could buy less for their money. It was the same as having some of the money taken away.

Isn't devaluation a form of stealing? Isn't it immoral?

A

The risk of inflation is inherent in the nature of paper money. And the risk will be greater the less hard cash backing the currency has.

People who save it ought to be aware of the risks involved and that money even in normal times will usually have some lessening in value. By saving it they naturally accept the risks. However, they have a right to expect a government to preserve a reasonable stability in the value of its currency. They are cheated when a government uses devaluation without honest necessity, say, to cover up mismanagement and experiments in foolish economic theories.

Q

Is there anything unfair in the labor-management relations between Catholic priests and their bishops?

I'm sure you know there's a good deal of unrest and un-
happiness among many priests. They feel there's something
unfair about the way they're ruled, so unfair that they
recommend being a priest to no one. It's not the way it
should be. It should be a most happy life.

Any clue to any injustice?

A

From my observations, the Catholic priest seems to be in
a position somewhat analogous to a man who is trained as
a civil engineer, wants to be a civil engineer, makes his living as a civil engineer but is forced to work for his first employer and under the latter's terms or never work as a civil
engineer at all. Of course, the engineer could leave his job
and find some other type of work; yet he would be unhappy
and at a great disadvantage because he has had no training
for anything else. So it is with the priest, except he also has
a stigma to overcome should he leave the priesthood for other
work. In general, therefore, he seems caught in a position
very much like an indentured servant who has little or no recourse if his master proves unreasonable.

How did he get into such an oppressive situation? By the
nature of Catholic belief the Church's authority is monarchi-
cal. This means the bishop has rather absolute power, and
rightly so, over the priest as a priest. But because the priest's
livelihood has slipped into being tied to his functioning as a
priest—practically no bishop ordains anymore except under
the supplementary title of "service of the diocese" (c.981
#1)—the bishop's autocratic power now extends over the
priest not only as a priest but also as a man.

This unjust situation was not meant to be. According to
Canon Law the priest ordinarily is to be given a benefice at
ordination. A benefice amounts to a livelihood befitting a
priest's position in the community (c.979). It is guaranteed
for life and could not be lost except for the grave reasons expressed in Canon Law (cc. 2299#3, 2302-5, 2280). Through the

financial independence it gave him, the priest gained a counterbalance to the autocratic power of the bishop so that the bishop could not push him around like a serf but had to treat him as a fraternal, team member. The bishop, on his part, had to pick his team of priests wisely for he had little financial room for error.

In my opinion, a return to some form of that financial independence is necessary. Associations of priests and the like can never do the trick without infringing on the rightful authority of the bishop.

Q

Is bankruptcy allowable?

What's the morality of bankruptcy? Can a person wipe out his debts that way and get a fresh start? I know it's legal, but is it moral? It seems to be cheating the people who loaned things.

A

Morally people should be allowed to get out from under an impossible burden that keeps them from producing enough to support themselves and their dependents. However, the relief that bankruptcy brings does not morally wipe out the debt but simply cancels it temporarily until the bankrupt can pay without impoverishing himself. Total release from the debt is only by the voluntary condonation of the creditors.

Since the bankruptcy laws in the United States, as I am told, favor complete freedom, a strong argument can be made that all debts are contracted under the implied condition that they will be condoned in case of bona fide bankruptcy. Unless that argument can be disproved, bona fide bankrupts in the U. S. are free to consider even their moral obligations discharged.

Chapter 4
Crime and Punishment

Q

May prisoners be allowed to unionize?

Do prisoners have a moral right to unionize?

A

Having proved irresponsible in the use of their rights prisoners can now be deprived of them. For example, since they cannot be trusted to vote for the benefit of the community, they can be denied the right to vote. Since, too, they should not be allowed to defeat the community's purpose in sending them to prison, they should not be allowed into a position where they can decide their punishment, the makeup of the parole board, their type of food, recreation, pay, and so forth; in other words, they should not be allowed to organize into a union.

Q

Is rehabilitation the purpose of prisons?

I am extremely alarmed at the unchristian nature of your answer to the question about prisoners having a moral right to unionize. You said that if prisoners could organize and make the decisions about the conditions of their confinement, they would be defeating the community's purpose in sending them to prison.

I ask: If people are sent to prison for rehabilitation, shouldn't they learn to make decisions for themselves so that when they get out they'll know how to live lawfully within a community?

A

Prisons are primarily for punishment. Fear of again being punished tends naturally to discourage law violations in the future; in other words, it tends to back people into rehabilitation.

As far as reasonably possible prisons also ought to use the positive approach to rehabilitation and try to instill virtue. But they are far less capable of handling that job than parents, schools, churches and society at large who were not able to succeed. Hence, they should be careful about wasting time and money on the impossible.

Prisoners already know what they must do to live lawfully; their problem comes in choosing to do so.

Q

Are poverty, grime and ignorance the sole causes of crime?

Swedish social engineers work on the theory that poverty, grime, overcrowding and ignorance are the causes of crime. They even attribute the bank holdup in Stockholm where the desperadoes kept four hostages in a vault for five days to the fault of society and not of the desperadoes. They think that once poverty and ignorance are eliminated, crime will be eliminated. Yet Sweden, where the standard of

*living for everyone is very high because of social welfare,
has a frightening big increase in crime.*

Any answer?

A

Sound philosophy is essential for sound social planning.
Without a correct analysis of man's nature, any social theory
is quite worthless. But the Swedish social engineers are
working on the erroneous supposition that man is purely a
material being (essentially no different from apes, dogs,
chickens) who, naturally, cannot have a free-will. As a consequence they think that man is completely subject to Pav-
lovian conditioned reflexes: change his environment for
the better and he will necessarily act more virtuously.

Man, though, is a material-immaterial combination. He
has an immaterial intellect and free-will which environment can only indirectly influence; he always remains fundamentally free to go against his surroundings, education,
psychotherapy and everything else and do exactly what he
wants—as good parents know who have an erring son. The
most learned and richest man in the world can still be a
villain.

Social engineers ought to see that everyone has the material necessities without which he finds it extremely difficult to be good; yet they must recognize man's inherent
freedom and realize that the affluence of society cannot
force him to be virtuous and that only a type of persuasion
will work, a persuasion through education, example of
heroes, hope of reward and fear of punishment.

Q

May police trap a drug pusher by posing as a buyer?

*Do police have a right to trap a person into criminal
action? I mean like posing as a buyer of dope in order to
catch the pusher.*

A

The police have no right to encourage a person to commit crime, no right to be the instigators of crime. Yet they can pose as a passive cooperator in crime in order to flush out suspected criminals. They can pretend to be a buyer of dope but only in a way that would test without encouraging the suspect's criminal determination. They could let it be known, for instance, that they wanted to buy; yet they should not so entreat him to sell that under the circumstances they might be pushing an honest, although weak man into crime.

Q

Ought there to be criminal sanctions against sexual acts performed in private between two consenting adults?

Isn't it wrong to have criminal sanctions against sexual acts performed in private between two consenting adults? Shouldn't adults be free to do whatever they want as long as they're not hurting anyone?

A

The community should want to prevent as far as possible her citizens from stooping to acts of homosexuality, bestiality and the like. Such acts give in to a depravity that runs counter to the virtues necessary for civilization and eats away at the strength of a nation. By having laws against unnatural sex even though the laws cannot be closely enforced, the community at least inhibits the acts somewhat through fear of getting caught and at the same time prevents the depraved from boldly parading their depravity and thereby encouraging others.

Q

Do criminals have a duty to make restitution?

A Miami judge is thinking about sentencing a second-degree murderer to supporting his victim's widow and five children instead of spending life in prison. The defense attorney described the judge's idea as a fresh approach worth thinking about; but the prosecution said it was "disgusting, abhorrent and abominable."

Which way morality?

A

A murderer has a moral duty to compensate for the harm the murder caused people other than the victim. He is bound, for instance, to do what he can to supply the financial support the victim gave his dependents. So, in that regard, the judge's idea is excellent.

Restitution, though, is not punishment. But punishment is needed for the defense of the tranquil order which is peace; it upholds the force of law, for without sanctions law could have no teeth. Hence, a murderer must not only be made to compensate for the harm he did but also suffer punishment for having broken the law.

Q

Should criminals be set free when the police gathered the convicting evidence illegally?

In 1961 the Supreme Court decided that evidence obtained by "unreasonable search and seizure" cannot be used in a trial. It's known as the "exclusionary rule" and was considered the way of making police respect the laws and not use wire-taps, illegal break-ins and so on. Yet under it

*a lot of criminals caught red-handed have been allowed to
go free.*

*Reversing the Court's ruling has been suggested, but
wouldn't that encourage the police to disregard the law
when they thought the end justified the means?*

A

A suspect's guilt depends on the facts. Facts are facts
legally or illegally obtained. If the facts prove him guilty, he
must be punished or else justice is not served and the community loses respect for it.

The person who broke the law to get the evidence must in
turn be held liable to punishment for his act. However, it
would be a perverse sense of justice, typical of a petulant
child, to consider his punishment as the freeing of the
criminal.

Q

Does justice require the "Miranda card"?

*The "Miranda card" contains the warning the police
must give the suspect they arrest. It details the suspect's
right to remain silent, to have an attorney, etc. As far as
justice is concerned, is it a milestone or a millstone?*

A

The rights of the defendant are given to help him avoid
being unjustly condemned. His right to remain silent, for
instance, prevents interrogators from forcing a confession
of guilt from an innocent man. The rights are not given to
help him escape justice. He is free to use them for that purpose only because the community cannot prevent him from
doing so.

Since justice is the purpose of the rights, the defendant

should be told of them and even required to use them when he otherwise would be in danger of unjust condemnation. Ordinarily, though, there is not that danger; and justice is best served by the defendant's full and uninhibited cooperation. Hence the police ordinarily ought to do nothing to prevent cooperation, say, by reminding him of his right to remain silent, to speak only through an attorney, and so forth. Their job is to serve justice, not to suggest ways of thwarting her. The thwarting they must let the defendant do for himself.

Q

May rapists be castrated?

Evangelist Billy Graham was once quoted as saying: "I think that a person found guilty of rape should be castrated. That would stop him pretty quick."

Morally wouldn't that punishment be inhumane and immoral?

A

Rape can be an extremely serious offense, at times resulting in the psychological death of the victim and therefore quite readily warranting, in my judgment, the death penalty. Even the average case demands severe punishment, and the more prevalent the crime the more severe the punishment ought to be.

Since a person who has committed a grave crime like murder can have his head chopped off without offense to morality or humaneness, he can have a less important part of his body cut away for an equal or less grave crime. Hence, any case of rape that would warrant the death penalty or anything relatively close to it would certainly justify castration.

Perhaps even the average case justifies castration. But before a community would install such punishment, she ought to make sure that she is not culpably contributing to the crime to any considerable extent. She may be at some fault, for instance, inasmuch as she allows nudity and outright pornography which get men "all steamed up."

Q

Ought an 8-year-old to be tried in a criminal court?

Is it morally right to try an 8-year-old in a criminal court like an adult as Scotland did recently?

A

Normally a child of eight years lacks the usual adult's realization of the evilness of crime and often acts thoughtlessly, impetuously and without the self-control which an adult is expected to have. Because he cannot be expected to act as responsibly as an adult, ordinarily he should not be tried and punished as one.

Q

Should the police play a benefit game against a homosexual organization?

Not long ago the police of San Francisco played a benefit baseball game against a homosexual organization. The proceeds went to send children (little boys no doubt) to summer camp.

Did the cops have a right to honor the lavender swishes like that even though it was for a good cause?

A

Homosexuality is a grave moral evil and very corruptive of the strength of the community. It ought to be suppressed as far as possible. Suppression, though, would not call ordinarily for hunting down the offenders; yet it would be intolerant of open display of their acts and organizations.

The San Francisco police were unfortunately not only tolerating an immoral organization but actually honoring it. The fact, too, that the game was played for a good cause did not lift, in my judgment, the prohibition that should have been there. Summer camp for a small group of boys was not that imperative that it compensated for the softening of the community's conscience against homosexuality; furthermore, the camp could have been arranged through harmless means.

Q

Shouldn't punishments be lenient rather than severe?

It's commonly agreed that long prison terms tend to alienate inmates from the norms of society and merely delay the recurrence of crimes for many prisoners.

Doesn't that argue against the severity of penalties as a means of more effective law enforcement?

A

A slap on the wrist for armed robbery makes the crime from the criminal's view worth committing and even encourages him in the crime since it shows how little the community thinks of the offense. On the other hand, being punished with death for throwing an empty beer bottle out the car window is preposterously unjust. Punishment must fit the crime, erring neither in leniency nor severity.

Imprisonment, of course, is only one form of punishment.

It could well be the wrong type for certain criminals, or be administered poorly. In either case it could be unnecessarily provoking alienation of the inmates from the norms of society. From such faulty imprisonment, though, no argument can be made against severity of penalties.

From my observations, I suspect that some prisons should be places of detention and nothing more. Like for the man awaiting trial who cannot be released on bail yet does not deserve punishment since he has not been convicted of any wrong. They should be little more than that, too, for people convicted of misdemeanors. But for hardened criminals they should not be play pens. Criminals should be made to work for their living, preferably at tasks the community finds necessary but repugnant; and by no means ought they to be allowed the usual civil rights of people on the outside.

Q

Is flogging moral?

A sheriff blocked a judge's order to flog a jail inmate who was convicted of assaulting a fellow inmate and creating a jail disturbance. The sheriff called the 15 lashes a "cruel, illegal sentence."

The judge was disappointed and termed the sheriff's action "a damn shame."

Morally, who's correct?

A

The right to life, which includes the right to be free of any aggression against the body, carries with it the correlative duty of living life fittingly. The murderer does not live fittingly but sheds his dignity as a human by acting as an unreasonable, dangerous, wild beast. By disavowing his humanity he forfeits his right to life, which forfeiture can be claimed by the community for her protection. So, too, a lesser criminal can rightly suffer corporal punishment less than death. Just as mothers spank their erring children, so the community can take a whip to erring adults.

Neither the community nor the mother is cruel. Neither takes delight in handing out punishment. Rather, each is showing her love by caring enough to correct the disorder.

Q

Should laws always be applied equally?

Some people have said the Watergate affair may divide the nation and bring down our form of government. It has already hurt the stock market and our relations with foreign countries. But don't we have to let the chips fall where they may and apply the law to everyone alike, big and small?

A

In justice laws cannot be applied irrespective of circumstances. Laws are norms fitting only the general run and not every conceivable set of circumstances. They require a judge to take the variables into consideration.

The application of the law is meant to achieve good, to uphold the peaceful order that should be in the community. If the application under a particular set of circumstances would be more disruptive than constructive, more harmful than beneficial to the community, the law ought not to be applied.

Thus, it could be that a president of the United States would be an outright petty crook who is caught in the act of lifting a wallet for the $50 in it. Now, the loss of respect for authority that that act if known by the general public would bring could be far more harmful to the community than allowing the theft to remain relatively secret and unpunished. So perhaps the president would have to be exempted from public prosecution in that case.

Whether Watergate was criminally a small matter and should have been taken care of secretly for the sake of the country, I leave to your judgment.

Q

Does the death penalty deter crime?

A Canadian government study said the death penalty does not prevent murder. It admitted the homicide rate has gone up since Canada suspended capital punishment for most crimes; yet the man who prepared the study said that the rise was due to the "general increase in criminal violence" and "would have taken place anyway even though the death penalty had not been suspended."

Doesn't that contradict what you've said about capital punishment deterring crime?

A

The study admits the homicide rate has gone up since capital punishment was suspended. That, of course, supports my contention that the fear of death is a deterrent to crime. The "general increase in criminal violence" is, I suggest, also due partially to the lack of strong, swift, sure punishment for crime.

Anyone denying the general efficacy of fear as a force for or against an activity cannot but have giant blind-spots in his analysis of human behaviour. He ought to be aware of his error merely from every day occurrences. A driver late for work often keeps within the speed limit solely because of his fear of getting a ticket; the married man having an affair sneaks around lest he be reported to his wife; the youngster crawls in his bedroom window so he will not be caught disobeying the curfew. Fear helps to keep us on the straight and narrow by backing us onto it when we are not virtuous enough to stay on it willingly. Ordinarily, too, the greater the punishment we fear, the greater the wrong we are being warned to avoid.

The greatest punishment normally is loss of life. In a sense, when life is gone, all is gone. Naturally, therefore, capital punishment is the ultimate deterrent and for that reason a splendid servant of the law against homicide and a powerful protector of life.

Q

Should kidnap victims be ransomed?

Do you have suggestions, morally, for dealing with kidnappers of foreign business executives? Lately a number of them have been kidnapped in Argentina and held for huge ransoms. If the ransom is paid, kidnapping is encouraged; if the ransom is not paid, kidnapping may be discouraged but the individual held may never live to appreciate that fact. Bodyguards for every individual who may be kidnapped are impossible.

A

The community's good must, as a rule, be chosen over the individual's good. Hence, to keep the entire community safe from kidnappings ransom ordinarily ought not to be paid so that kidnapping will be shown a useless effort. Kidnappers themselves should be pursued relentlessly and punished swiftly and severely. And by no means should they be allowed to use the courts as a sounding board for propaganda.

Every citizen must have the courage to suffer for the common good when necessary. If he lacks the courage, he does not deserve to live in a free society.

Q

Should the press detail methods of crime and the counter-measures of law enforcers?

A newspaper editorial criticized a man from the Federal Bureau of Investigation for accusing the press of aiding air piracy by publicizing details of skyjackers' methods and the countermeasures of law enforcers. It said the press has no business on the law enforcement's "team" or on the law-breaker's "team" but should be on the public's "team," because the function of the press is to dig out the news and to print it for the public.
Who's correct?

A

The law enforcement's "team" is the public's "team." The public is obliged to help keep public order and therefore to cooperate with its official law enforcers.

As far as it went the criticism of the F.B.I. man was correct: detailing how to skyjack and how to avoid being caught, like publicizing the combination of the local bank vault, cannot but help the criminal mind. Normally such details should not be given unless there is a proportionate good to be gained.

Q

Is amnesty for military deserters moral?

I've heard that amnesty for military deserters is not a legal but a moral issue. If that is true, then you should have a solution?

A

Citizens who desert rather than fulfill their duty of defending their country are parasites who would enjoy benefits without shouldering responsibilities. In the abstract, the community has every right to brush them off or punish them if they remain in the country.

Circumstances, though, like the greatness of the number of deserters, little culpability, probability of slight harm if amnesty were granted, could allow a community to grant pardon.

The basic principles of amnesty concern justice and are therefore a matter of morality. But the application of the principles in concrete circumstances belongs to prudential judgment.

Q

What can be done to improve the American penal system?

The American penal system is now thought to be a major breeder of crime. Prisons lock men away from their families, jobs, and normal living and breed hatred, despair, alienation, and, consequently, crime.

Some suggested remedies are to decriminalize offenses like alcoholism, drug abuse, adult-consenting sexual acts, gambling, and by so doing prevent a lot of people from going to prison; to change the bail system so people won't go to jail because they can't raise the bail money; to allow the criminal to live on the outside but with his work and leisure monitored so that he has "restricted freedom."

Any suggestions of your own?

A

Decriminalizing crime or giving law violators the tender care reserved for sick children is no solution. Crime must be punished or else peace within the community falls apart; and it must be punished in proportion to the harm that freedom to commit that crime would do the community (the degree of punishment declares how much the community abhors the crime).

Only one suggestion will I make here. It is for a return to a traditional form of punishment.

This punishment would not be applicable to all law violators but it would to a great many who otherwise would go to prison. It would not tear them from their families, jobs, and community, or force them into a long, close association with hardened criminals. It would neither breed crime nor would its cost be felt by the community. It would be a penalty proportionate to the crime and nothing for the penalized to be proud of. Of course it would be moral.

Let me whisper it lest the theorists of non-violence tear me apart: *Corporal punishment.*

Chapter 5

Death and Life

Q

When does life begin?

When does man's life begin? Is it at the moment of fertilization of the ovum as most anti-abortionists believe?

A

The traditional, philosophical argument for man's life beginning at the moment of fertilization centers around the theory that the "form" of the material being, which gives the body life and guides it through development, must be one and the same throughout the being's existence. But since the "form" of the developed man is demonstrably the intellectual soul, that soul must be present from the moment of fertilization and that moment must mark the beginning of man's life as a human with all his rights.

However, I am inclined to deny the need for a material being having one and the same soul throughout its existence. Rather I think Aquinas was correct in saying, "At first the embryo has a soul which is merely sensitive (capable of sense perception) and when this is taken away, it is supplanted by a more perfect soul which is both sensitive and intellectual." (*Summa*, I, q. 76, a.3, ad 3. For an elaboration of the point: I, q. 118, a. 2, ad 2.)

It is certain, of course, that an intellectual soul is immaterial and subsistent and therefore cannot be generated; it can only be created. A sensitive soul, though, can be generated. Now, it seems to me that a sensitive soul, generated by humans, would suffice for human bodily development; then, after the brain developed sufficiently, the sensitive soul would be supplanted by an intellectual one bringing human life.

For one thing, it seems unreasonable that an intellectual soul which needs a material brain for its peculiar activity would be present before the brain would be usable even for the most rudimentary tasks. But without an activity peculiar to itself, the soul would have no sufficient reason for existence and therefore could not exist.

The fact, too, that identical twins are formed by the splitting of what was once a one-cell, fertilized ovum argues against the one-cell zygote having an intellectual soul. After all, an intellectual soul can neither co-inform the same body with another intellectual soul nor be split into two.

Also, the supplanting of a less perfect soul for the more perfect is consonant with the theory, which seems to be definitely true, that brain death constitutes the death of man. Except the process is in reverse. When the body can no longer be useful to the intellectual soul, that soul leaves; yet the body still accommodates a less perfect soul capable, at least, of nourishment.

Supplanting also appears to be accepted on principle by traditional theologians who rather unanimously allow for a limited evolution. They work on the supposition that if evolution were a fact and man evolved from an animal, the souls of a male and female near-human animal were finally supplanted by two intellectual souls and the resulting two persons became the parents of us all.

Furthermore, scientists Arthur Hertig and John Rock tell us, and their statements seem to be generally accepted as scientifically accurate, that 58% of all fertilized human eggs are lost within the first two weeks. They simply do not make it down the fallopian tubes or are not properly implanted on the wall of the uterus. (Later some 11% more are lost. Only 31% actually come to birth.) Now it seems unbecoming God's providence that all those one-cell and few-celled beings which are lost should be immortal humans.

If my conclusions are correct, then direct, intentional abortion at the earliest stages of development would not be the moral evil of murder but of illicit birth control.

Q

May mongoloid babies be allowed to die?

If a newly born infant has severe mental retardation, "mongoloid" features and a block in his intestinal tract which will cause him to starve to death unless the block is taken care of by a simple operation, do the parents have a moral option of having the operation or letting the child die and end his short life as an abnormal human?

A

The parents are bound to take ordinary care of the child. So your question really is: Given the abnormal circumstances of the child, is the simple operation ordinary or extraordinary care?

Apparently the only trouble with the child other than the block of his intestinal tract which you say can be taken care of by a simple operation (which I take to mean a run-of-the-mill, low-risk operation) is his mental retardation. But the retardation is not causing him suffering and making his life miserable interminably. On the contrary, mongoloids are usually very happy, loveable people, capable, too, of simple tasks. Besides, the extent of the mental retardation of mongoloids cannot be determined with any great accuracy within the time it would be imperative for the child to have the operation.

Under the circumstances, then, it would seem that the child should be treated very much like any other child and the operation considered ordinary care.

Q

Should the American Medical Association accept "mercy killing" as a policy?

In commenting on a case in New York where a doctor was charged with murder for having injected a lethal poison into an incurably sick patient, Dr. Malcolm Todd, the then president-elect of the American Medical Association, gave the impression in a newspaper interview that the AMA may soon be willing to accept "mercy killing" as a policy. He said the policy should not leave the decision on "mercy killing" to the attending physician alone but only in conjunction with a consulting board or panel.

Shouldn't the man and his relatives be consulted too?

A

The direct, intentional killing of an innocent person is murder. But since sickness is no crime and does not change innocence to guilt, the patient can neither kill himself nor be killed by others. Thus, any move by Dr. Todd, the AMA, or anyone else towards the implementation of euthanasia is highly immoral.

The human fittingness of euthanasia is a matter of morality. Just as moralists as such are no more qualified to act as physicians than the local plumber, so too physicians as such are not qualified as moralists. Physicians, it seems, often fail to recognize that fact.

Q

May the mentally ill and deformed be put to death?

I see absolutely no logical reason why the mentally ill, the physically deformed and the very aged, all who are unable to care for themselves, should not be put out of their plight by painless gassing or injections. This would be mercy killing with a capital "M".

A

Human life belongs to God. Consequently, as a pilot captains his airliner under the supervision of the owner company so man must care for human life under God's supervision.

Killing an innocent person directly and intentionally is murder and horrendously against the Creator's rules. But mercy killing, as I said previously, does not escape the definition of murder. Suffering does not strip a man of innocence.

Nor is suffering the absolute evil you seem to think it is. Certainly in one sense it is an evil, but in another sense it can be far more productive of good than pleasure can.

Q

Are drinking and smoking forms of suicide?

I know self-destruction is wrong. But doesn't drinking and smoking bring on a slow suicide? Aren't they as immoral as putting a bullet through one's head?

A

For an adequate reason, like saving his country or a fellow man, a person may accept death; and for a lesser reason, a lessening of his life span. To earn a livelihood, for instance, he may take considerable risks and work in a mine or chemical factory, or as a steeplejack, prizefighter and so on. Even to enjoy life he is free to risk harm—provided that the risk is proportionate to the good he receives. No pleasure, though, would compensate for stepping with certainty into lung cancer or cirrhosis of the liver.

Q

May people risk their lives in dare-devil stunts?

Does a person have the right to take his life in his hands and do dare-devil stunts like the motorcyclist who plans on jumping the Grand Canyon?

A

Man has a right to risk his life for a proportionate good. Soldiers, coal miners, bullfighters, policemen, firemen, anyone driving a car or flying, in fact all of us are constantly risking our lives in some degree or other.

The dare-devil who through his risks earns his living (which is a great good) is free to take greater risks than the man who would do stunts merely for thrills. He may not play Russian roulette, but he may rely upon his skill to see him safely through circumstances which the unskilled could not tackle without death or injury. Thus the high-wire artist may perform without a safety net when his skill would normally see him safely across and his livelihood or a similar good relatively requires the risk. The same general principles apply also to the motorcyclist who would leap the Grand Canyon.

Q

May a person be nailed to a cross as a means of demonstrating for world peace?

In Santo Domingo a man had himself nailed to a cross in a demonstration for world peace and love. After some 24 hours the doctors said he should come off the cross because of a foot infection. His wife then had herself nailed to the cross to continue the demonstration.

Is it moral to demonstrate that way?

A

A person being dragged to death because of a hand caught in a machine could cut the member off to save his life. But such intentional maiming is only allowable when (1) it is intrinsically related to the good effect, (2) there is no alternative, less harmful way of achieving the good, (3) the good is reasonably certain of being achieved and (4) is greater than the harm. Injuring the body intentionally as a means of demonstration seems, therefore, to be ruled out. It is neither intrinsically related to the goal nor is it the only way of attaining it.

Q

When is a person dead?

A man was shot in the head. Doctors said his brain was damaged so extensively that he would never again have brain activity, and they pronounced him dead. Yet they kept his heart and other organs functioning until his heart was taken for a transplant.

The man accused of the victim's murder claimed the vic-

tim did not die from the bullet wound but from the removal of the heart.

When is a person dead?

A

Death is the absence of life. So the basic question in the definition becomes: What is life? (The answer belongs primarily to philosophy, not to the empirical science of medicine.)

Life is the ability to move oneself. (Movement must not be understood as confined simply to local motion. Thinking also is motion.) The principle of life, the fundamental source responsible for animating a being, is customarily denominated the soul. Every living creature—carrot, dog, man—must have a soul; and the moment the soul ceases its union with the body, the creature is dead.

Now, man has a higher type soul than a carrot or dog. His is intellectual. Its reason for existence is intellectual activity. For its activity in this life it needs the use of a material brain. But when the brain can no longer be used, the intellectual soul no longer has reason to be united with the body; so the union ceases and the man is dead. Brain death, then, is the death of the man. As long as the brain remains capable of the least intellectual activity, the man is alive even though the functions of his heart, lungs and liver have been taken over by machines.

Determining when the brain in the physical reality is so extensively and irreversibly damaged that there can no longer be the least intellectual activity is the job of neurologists and their like. They still depend, though, on philosophy for a complete delineation of intellectual activity.

Q

May a mother turn off the respirator on her child who has suffered brain death?

In Denver a mother ordered doctors to turn off the respirator keeping her 10 year-old son alive. The boy had been struck by a car and was in a coma. The doctors said his brain was dead and he could never regain consciousness.

Did the mother have a right to order the respirator turned off?

A

Brain death, as I reasoned in the previous answer, is the death of the individual person. Therefore, if the doctors were correct in their diagnosis, the boy was truly dead despite the fact that his lungs and heart were still working. The mother did nothing more than put a quietus to the two organs.

Even though someone erred and the boy were still alive, yet since he had no chance of recovery and his life depended upon extraordinary means of support, his mother was within her moral right to refuse the means.

Q

Is a boy with two heads one or two people?

A boy with two heads was born recently in Buenos Aires. Each head seemed to be independent of the other. When one leg was pinched the head on that side of the body would cry but the other would not. The boy died after a few days.

Would you say the boy was one or two persons?

A

From your brief description, the "boy" probably was two boys. The fact that both heads were living and reacting as distinct entities indicates that there were two brains and an intellect to use each brain. And where there is an intellect, there is a person.

A human can do without arms, legs, and almost everything except a head. When his brain dies, he dies.

Q

Does life exist on Mars?

The latest pictures of Mars have given some evidence that water once flowed on the planet and increased the possibility that some kind of life exists there. The conclusion is based on the assumption that chemical evolution is the process which started life.

If life is present on Mars, will Martians be bound by our morality?

A

Fundamentally all intelligent creatures are bound by the same general morality which calls for them to love God, themselves and their neighbors. However, specific acts against love will vary according to the nature of the intelligent creatures. For instance, if a group were immortal, murder would naturally not be a problem. The same would be said of adultery, fornication and the like if a group were without sex.

Whether we have to be concerned about Martians or life on any planet besides Earth is a question I would be inclined to answer in the negative.

From reason we can argue that all life short of intelligent life exists for intellectual, material beings. Without the latter the former would have no reason for existing. Hence, unless there is intelligent life or its potential on a planet, there are no lesser forms of life—germs, plants, fish, animals—on the planet. An exception could be possible, though, if the lower life would be somehow necessary on one planet to sustain or enhance intellectual life on another. The chance of this necessity as far as Earth is concerned seems very remote.

We can also argue that all intelligent beings struggling towards their final goal have a certain dependency upon each other. All other intelligent beings who have gone through their test either aid or obstruct the strugglers. But traditionally the entire economy of salvation has been known to be concerned only with Earthlings, good and bad angels, and God. It would seem, therefore, that God would have been deficient in His instruction to us if He had omitted telling us about another world of people who had a bearing on our lives.

Chapter 6
Privacy and Secrets

Q

Do long range cameras lower the barriers to rightful privacy?

Do photographers with their long range cameras have a right to pry into people's privacy like they did some time ago to Jackie Kennedy Onassis? They used scuba equipment to get within range as she sunned herself in the nude on her private beach.

A

People against whom there is no reasonable suspicion of law violation have a right to privacy. To use that right they need only to take the ordinary, natural measures for assuring privacy. Lowering their voice when in public so under normal conditions only the intended can hear, leaving public places and going into secluded areas where walls and distances protect them from the natural eye and ear power of the unwelcome, and so forth. People cannot be obliged to take more than such simple means of assuring privacy, otherwise there would be no end to their lack of privacy because of the ingenuity of snoopers and the ever increasing advancement in electronic eavesdropping and peeping aids.

Photographers must accept this limitation to their filming. Seemingly in Jackie's case they overstepped the line.

Q

Are computerized data banks on citizens an invasion of privacy?

Credit agencies and government have been computer-storing more and more information on individual citizens. Instinctively I don't like it. I'm afraid the information can be used against us by a "Big Brother" someday.
What's the moral angle?

A

Although a man may have nothing shamefacedly to hide, he should be able to have a privacy which respects his right to direct his own search for happiness and fulfillment. Living a fish bowl existence puts him at the mercy of the onlookers. He is open to having his plans blocked, discoveries stolen, personal associations inhibited, moments of relaxation ridiculed, and so on. He needs privacy to preserve his dignity as a human responsible for his own life. Hence, data banks of any type which would destroy rightful privacy should not be permitted.

Even the ordinary buyer making a purchase at a clothing shop has a right to have his purchases and any file the shop may keep on him kept confidential. The shop violates that trust by giving or selling his file to other shops or, worse yet, to an agency which would collate a composite picture of him. The agency, of course, would be compiling a bank of data which could be so vast that it could easily approach the intimate knowledge of the person which only a psychiatrist would be expected to have. Obviously such information in the wrong hands could be devastatingly harmful; and there would be no reason as far as the person is concerned for the agency to have the information any more than there would be, as far as a jewelry store is concerned, for an unknown man to possess its set of keys.

Q

Does the President have a right to record secretively the conversations in his White House offices?

Since 1971 President Richard Nixon had been recording conversations and telephone calls taking place in his offices. Senators, foreign diplomats and everyone who entered were usually recorded "for history" although, I suppose, they didn't know about it and thought they were dealing with the President alone and in confidence.

Morally was the President right in setting up the "bug"?

A

Privacy is a bulwark of freedom. For freedom's sake people have a right to keep their activities secret as long as they are not causing unjust harm. They have a right to consult in confidence or simply to hold an everyday conversation with a person without others listening in. But, ordinarily, recording secretly a conversation for those others to hear at a later time is merely another form of eavesdropping and an immoral breach of the right to privacy.

Recording "for history" is no excuse.

Q

May the internal affairs of another nation be meddled with?

In the face of awful reprisals from his government Andrei Sakharov, a physicist who helped develop the Soviet H-bomb, warned the West about accepting a detente with Russia on Russia's terms because the West being disarmed would suddenly find herself confronted by Russia armed to the teeth. Sakharov suggested that the West's economic leverage be used to force a democratization of Russia. Denying trade concessions to countries that restrict emigration would be a "minimum step."

His idea sounds reasonable but isn't it wrong to interfere in the internal affairs of another country?

A

Forcing a government to allow its people to exercise their natural human rights is not wrong interference. Rather, there is a duty to interfere just as there is a duty to force bandits to free their hostages.

Internal affairs correctly reserved to a ruling government are restricted to those that are in accord with natural, human rights. Thus, a government acts within its jurisdiction when it seeks to regulate emigration, speech, property ownership, etc. with all other demands of justice; on the other hand, it acts not only outside its jurisdiction but unjustly when it denies the basic freedoms of emigration, speech, and so forth.

Q

May the government search every citizen boarding an airliner?

Does the government have the right to search every citizen before he boards an airliner? I know hijacking is a problem, but isn't indiscriminate searching of everyone one of the things our forefathers fought the British over?

A

Government has a right to make reasonable searches. Ordinarily the reasonableness is assured through the requirement of a search warrant issued by an unbiased third party, the judiciary.

A general type of search warrant is rightly in effect for everyone passing through customs. Seemingly, too, a general warrant can be put on in time of an emergency like the present hijacking scare.

Of course this breach of the airline passengers' privacy is an evil that should be avoided if possible. I personally think the same effect can and should be had by other means— mainly a hard stance by government, which might risk a few lives but would end hijacking without the waste of resources and the conditioning of people towards accepting less and less privacy.

Q

May a possibly incriminating bullet be dug from the suspect's body?

During a supermarket holdup in Indiana a policeman was killed, but before he died he wounded one of the fleeing bandits. A tip from an informer led police to the wounded bandit. Under a court order the bullet fragments were surgically removed and expert witnesses later testified that the bullet came from the slain officer's gun. The bandit was convicted and sentenced to life imprisonment.

On appeal, though, the Indiana Supreme Court freed the murderer because, it said, his rights had been violated by removing the bullet without his consent.

Which court is correct?

A

A person's body is more inviolable than his home, but neither is absolutely inviolable. On reasonable suspicion a warrant can be gotten to search a suspect's home for stolen goods; border guards can even make a body search for contraband swallowed or hidden in an orifice. It seems merely an extension of that search to extract bullet fragments from the body of a suspected murderer.

Being a suspect means there is evidence pointing to his guilt. It is that connection with guilt which justifies, it seems to me, the troubles he may be put to without his consent while being investigated and awaiting trial—as long as the troubles are not disproportionate to the crime and the strength of the evidence against him. Hence, if the crime is grave enough and the evidence strong enough, morally he may be searched, subjected to a hammering of questions likely to cause him to blurt out the truth, denied bail, kept in prison, and so on even to extracting a bullet for evidence.

Q

May income tax records be given other agencies than the IRS?

A presidential order, later rescinded, opened the income-tax records of three million farmers to the inspection of the U. S. Department of Agriculture. If the records could be opened to Agriculture officials and not just to Treasury people checking on possible criminal violation, couldn't they be opened to any official of any department? And then how much privacy would we have?

Wasn't it proper to rescind the order because of the invasion of privacy?

A

Information required in tax reports ought generally to be kept at a minimum and once recorded kept as confidential as possible. If a tax system needs information that is uncomfortable in its extensiveness or dissemination, the system could well be unjust because of the invasion of privacy. The loss of privacy can be far more detrimental than the loss of efficiency in collecting taxes. The former leads to tyranny whereas the loss of some government revenues can even have its compensations: less paternalism and more adult responsibility for citizens.

In the light of those principles the order would seem difficult to defend.

Q

In general, what privacy do public figures have a right to?

Since the public has a right to know and since every bit of knowledge figures in estimating the worth of an elected government official, how much privacy does a person like the President of the United States have a right to?

A

The public's right to know (the other side of the public's duty to be informed) ordinarily does not supersede a person's right to privacy. The right to know merely gives people the right to gather information where and when they can without violating laws or infringing on anyone's rights.

The news-making government official has less right to privacy than the usual private citizen. Unlike the latter he cannot play the hermit. He has a duty to answer, within his expertise, questions that serve the public. Too, because almost his every action is relatively important to the public as a means of gauging his character and possible reactions to official problems, he has to allow a certain intrusion upon what for others would normally be part of private life. He has to recognize that he is constantly "on stage" even at a round of golf or at dinner in a restaurant. Yet he is human and does need some privacy. So, after he has reasonably taken care of his duty towards the public, he has a right to escape the insatiably curious by taking the ordinary means of secluding himself. For instance, by entering his home he should be free of attempts by outsiders to see and hear what goes on inside, or by expressly asking for privacy while on a morning stroll he should be free from the badgering of reporters.

Q

Should truth, no matter how unflattering, be said about the dead?

I read an article encouraging us to tell the truth about the dead even when it isn't flattering. I always thought the old saying, de mortuis nihil nisi bonum, *was pretty good. So why knock a man when he's dead?*

What's correct?

A

Ordinarily the evil a person does should not be made public unless the disclosure serves a good proportionate to the harm which would be done through the blackening of his reputation.

Having a good reputation while alive frequently helps a person to be good because of a fear of losing the reputation. Moreover, his good reputation encourages other people to follow his example and frees the community that much more from evil. Hence, blackening a person's character is by no means a small harm.

There is still less reason for relating the evil deeds of the dead. Sometimes, though, it may be necessary for historical perspective or, perhaps, to warn the naive from placing implicit trust in every buoyant, quick-witted, self-confident personality thrust into the limelight.

Q

May government seize the financial records of a citizen once he turns them over to his accountant?

Should the government be able to seize the private records of a taxpayer once he turns them over to an accountant? The U. S. Supreme Court voted in the affirmative against a restaurant owner from Roanoke, Va. But Justice William O. Douglas dissented and said that a taxpayer doing his own bookkeeping could invoke the Fifth Amendment and keep his records secret and therefore should be able to keep them secret too when he employs an accountant to help him.

How do you see it?

A

A taxpayer may not be forced to testify against himself. In that regard his memory and written memory aids are inviolable—to which the Supreme Court agrees.

But, contrary to the majority on the Court, it seems to me the taxpayer uses an accountant as an extension of his personal efforts and, therefore, his records in the accountant's hands should be as inviolable as they are in his own. Also, if that were not true, the taxpayer would be forced into the inefficiency of transporting the accountant and his office into his own home so the records could remain confidential. Laws, though, are meant to be helpful, not detrimental;

and confidentiality does not lessen through simply a change of location.

If without the power to subpoena records from accountants the government would be finagled out of a major part of her tax revenues, she ought to recognize the conflict as one of her own making. A solution lies in devising a simple tax system whereby the average intelligent person could correctly and without help figure his taxes to the penny and know that he did so.

Q

Must family secrets be kept?

Is it wrong for a son or an employee to write about unflattering family matters? I'm thinking of Elliott Roosevelt's shocking story of his parents' lives. There have been other books too by servants of big personages.

A

Anything that would injure or displease another person ordinarily must be kept secret. And that includes injuring the good reputation of the dead.

Family members are bound more strongly to the above ruling among themselves than they are towards outsiders since they are obliged to love the family more than outsiders. Servants, too, are bound more strongly because they are committed to a type of professional secrecy because through their occupation they, like doctors and lawyers, are in a position to know what otherwise would be secret.

Also, family members have a right to privacy, to relax and live in close association without having a reporter disguised as part of the family detailing everything to the public. That right is natural and should be respected unless the family decrees differently.

Q

May burglary ever be sanctioned?

Morally can the President sanction burglary, like the rifling of the files of Daniel Ellsberg's psychiatrist, for the sake of national security? Senator Sam Ervin implied strongly that the President cannot and, moreover, would be violating the Fourth Amendment.

A

Law which does not forbid an intrinsic evil like murder can be broken to obtain a greater good or prevent a greater evil. Such law usually can be written only for the general run of circumstances, not every contingency. And wise men recognize this.

To save someone from death, a rescuer may have to cross the street against the "Don't Walk" signal or commandeer a private automobile or break into a home. So, too, necessity may require the security forces of the community to break and enter and "burglarize" a suspect's home without going through the ordinary, legally expressed channels. There would be nothing unreasonable about such search and seizure and hence nothing against the Fourth Amendment.

Q

Are there limits to a psychiatrist's secrecy?

A rejected suitor, Prosenjit Poddar, told a University of California clinical psychologist the detailed plan of how he was going to kill the girl who had rejected him. The man meant every word. The psychologist and two psychotherapists agreed that he was undergoing "paranoid schizophrenic reaction, acute and severe" and would probably kill.

The immediate prescription was 72-hour emergency psy-

*chiatric detention for the troubled 25-year-old. And the
Berkeley police were so informed.*

*But Dr. Harvey Powelson, director of psychiatry at UC's
hospital countermanded the order and Poddar was allowed
the freedom to proceed with his planned murder. Soon af-
terwards he stabbed Tattiana Tarasoff to death with a 13-
inch breadknife.*

*Miss Tarasoff's parents sued Dr. Powelson and four police-
men for negligence and failure to take action knowing of
the killer's murderous mental state. But the appellate court
with Justice John Molinari presiding ruled (according to the
newspaper) that the psychologist's duty to keep secret the
information given by the patient took priority over warning
the potential victim.*

Was the court's ruling realistic?

A

Plans for doing unjust harm do not fall within the legitimate bounds of secrecy. The confidant accepts a secret only
on condition that it does not unjustly harm him or anyone
else. Thus no one planning a crime and looking for necessary confederates can exact a validly binding promise of
secrecy while interviewing for confederates. The inter-
viewed, in fact, are morally bound to disclose the secret
plans when disclosure is necessary for preventing the evil.

The above principles apply to psychiatrists and psycholo-
gists as well as to everyone else.

Q

May grand jury secrets be leaked?

*During the time of the leaking of grand jury evidence
against the then Vice-President Spiro Agnew, Newsweek
(Sept. 10, 1973) carried an article giving a solution to the
morality of the unlawful leaks. To its questions, Is Agnew*

entitled to the same protection that is available to ordinary citizens or is the information free to be leaked and printed in newspapers? it answered: The information is too important to the public; the Vice-President must cede his right to confidentiality. It also set the press "beyond the law" and gave editors the right to decide "when the 'right to know' outweighs the process of law."

Did you agree?

A

A grand jury seeks to determine whether the suspicions against a person appear justified enough to call for an indictment. In the process it checks out all evidence, including hear-say, which may have little connection with fact. The jury is naturally bound, therefore, to keep its suspicions and proceedings secret lest the suspect be unjustly defamed, and a promise of secrecy is rightly required of it by the community.

Now, since the jury proceedings constitute, as far as the community is concerned, a natural secret, they can be revealed by the community when revelation is necessary for avoiding considerable harm to herself or another. Whether the need for the information in Agnew's case rose to such proportion that the people had a right to it is a question perhaps for historians some twenty years from now when there probably would be a less bias-cluttered perspective.

However, it can be said that any citizen, news editors included, who takes upon himself to leak legally confidential information must convince the court that the law did not apply in his case or be prepared to suffer the consequences of the illegal action. The judgment of the individual cannot be substituted for that of the community.

Q

Was President Nixon morally correct in handing over Watergate tapes and transcripts?

If the Watergate tapes were confidential (conversations with advisors, etc.) as President Nixon stated, wasn't it immoral of him to give up the contents despite the political pressures?

A

Professional confidences, which the Watergate tapes seemed to have been, may not be revealed except by the consent of the people who did the confiding or, ordinarily, when revealing would be necessary for preventing unjust harm. They may not be broken for the sake of prosecuting past law-violations. The indefinite good that comes from punishing an illegal act cannot outweigh the certain, definite good of being able to have confidences kept.

Nixon faced rather predictable pressures.

Legal positivism is the philosophy of law permeating our country. It denies that nature determines whether an action is just or unjust and denies that nature gives man any inviolable, inalienable right; instead it holds that justice and rights are determined entirely by the vote of the people. (In theory, murder would be moral and just if the people voted it in.) Consequently, many of the courts, politicians and newsmen Nixon faced saw nothing wrong in pressuring him to give up confidential matter. In their opinion, the clamor of the people made things just.

Q

Do soldiers have a right to say anything they want in order to avoid torture?

After the last prisoner of war was released by North Vietnam and came home, the POWs began to tell about their tortures and how the enemy tried to wring "confessions" and denunciations of the United States from them. Many broke under the torture.

Our military code demands uncompromising resistance against intimidation. But wouldn't it be better for the military to allow soldiers to say anything they want when they get caught? That way the enemy would be deprived of any benefit from "confessions" because the world would know the captives were making the statement to avoid torture. At the same time it would make the soldier's life a lot easier; he'd be free of torture and the guilt feeling that breaking under torture causes.

A

If the soldiers are allowed to say anything they want when captured—to tell all plans and secrets, they would jeopardize (1) the lives of their buddies still fighting, (2) the effectiveness of their army and the good it seeks to accomplish, (3) possibly the very life of their country. Hence, a military code has to demand uncompromising resistance against intimidation.

As far as propaganda goes, a code that would allow captives to say anything they want would be a disaster. The people at home would have no way of knowing they were not sincere and would be inclined to lose heart and give up; dissenters, on the other hand, would have a field day.

The enemy must be made to respect the duty that captives have towards their country.

Chapter 7
Marriage and
No Marriage

Q

Does the marriage commitment require exclusivity?

My boy friend is a member of a rock group. He explains his extra love affairs as just part of the life style he's in. He says the girls mean nothing to him and I should understand. I don't think he will change when we marry.

Should I always forgive him?

A

In the marriage commitment the man and woman promise exclusive right over their bodies to one another. The exclusivity is required by nature for the sake of family unity and at the same time is implicit to the total giving naturally expressed by the sex act.

From your evidence, the boy friend is not ready for marriage. Nor would he, granting the continuation of his attitude, be able to contract a valid marriage.

Q

Must marriage vows be "for keeps"?

Ypsilanti, Michigan, has revamped the marriage vows pronounced by couples who marry before the city's mayor. It deleted "until death do you part" in recognition that marriages are no longer considered to last forever.

I may be old fashioned or something, but marriages that aren't "for keeps" seem to be immoral. Am I right or wrong?

A

By its nature marriage is a permanent union, a lifetime vow of unity. Only such a covenant between husband and wife properly meets the needs of the family and expresses the unity which the sex act implies.

If the marriage vows are temporary, there is no marriage. Morally it is simply an agreement to shack-up with some legal arrangements until one party wants out.

Q

Does deception about pregnancy invalidate the consequent marriage?

If a woman falsely tells a man she is pregnant to induce marriage, can that marriage rightly be annulled?

A

The contract of marriage has to be treated somewhat differently from the ordinary buying-selling contract. If marriage were simply the latter type of contract, few husbands and wives would be validly married since almost invariably there is some deception, some hiding of faults and pretending at virtue prior to their marriage. Hence, for the sake of avoiding the colossal harm that would come from continual, wholesale invalidations of marriages the usual deception over the quality of a person married—nobility, wealth, pregnancy, etc.—cannot serve as a cause of invalidation.

Q

Should 16 year-olds marry?

Do you think a boy is too young to marry at 16 and a girl at 15?

A

Ordinarily, at least in the United States and the Western world, 15- and 16-year-olds are just beginning to step into the problems of life which will help to develop them into mature people. They neither know themselves nor are capable of knowing another person well enough to come to a reasonable decision resulting in marriage. Of course, it is difficult for the young to see that they lack requisite maturity since their very lack prevents them from having the standard to judge by. Instead, they must trust in general the judgment of elders like their parents.

Q

Is foreplay allowable?

I was virginal at the time of my marriage and I fear all I knew was the basic physiological way of begetting babies. I felt that sex wasn't nice. I was not prepared for the more intimate foreplay that precedes the sexual act. I think now that I've been wrong; yet I still feel "violated" by the touch, caress or whatever is necessary to stimulate me to the desire of intercourse. I need reassurance that I've been wrong. I know how unhappy I must make my husband.

A

Sex outside of marriage is strictly forbidden, and all safeguards for preserving purity ought to be taken. Between husband and wife, though, there is nothing unchaste about sex that follows the course of nature; in fact, it is a good that should be used and enjoyed.

Foreplay is simply a part of sex, adding to its pleasure and satisfaction and hence to the bond uniting man and wife. So, do yourself and your husband a favor: relax and enjoy it.

Q

May there be a licensing for parenthood?

I know you're opposed to licensing for parenthood but I think it is the only realistic way of assuring proper care for children. Parents should know the rudiments of nutrition and education and child psychology and be free of hereditary defects, otherwise they should not be parents.

A

People who cannot meet the responsibilities of parenthood have a duty not to have children. (This does not mean they can take immoral means of avoiding children.) But the right to marry and have a family is a natural right and is not given by the state. The state may merely protect citizens by excluding from marriage those who are naturally incapable of the marriage contract because of the lack of age, sanity or physical ability to perform the marriage act. It is up to the people who are married to determine for themselves whether they can meet the responsibilities of parenthood and of caring for a possibly deformed child.

Q

May tax exemptions for children be lowered to keep the population down?

A White House tax policy committee came up with the advice that tax exemptions for large families should be lowered. It proposed exemptions of $2,000 for a couple, $600 for the first child, $400 for the second, and $200 for any others. Behind the thinking was the fear of overpopulation.

Some people assailed the plan as "discriminatory." How do you see it?

A

The second, third, fourth, etc. children are obviously discriminated against. But there is more at fault with the committee's plan than that—at least in my judgment: it seems to me the proposal runs counter to man's inherent right to marry and determine for himself within the natural and divine laws whether to have children, how many, and when.

Man's right to marry is prior to the state. He established the state to help protect such rights and allow him to use them to the fullest. He may not, therefore, be forbidden by the state to marry when he is capable of marriage or to have children once he is married.

For the sake of external order the state may express legally the requisites, like age and sanity, which must be met before a person can be considered capable of entering into a valid marriage contract. Once the person is married the state may encourage him with rewards to use his marital right and have children when an increase of population is advantageous to the community; but, in my opinion, it may do no more than advise him not to have children when an increase is disadvantageous. For if the state went further and imposed the least penalty on his use of his marital right, on principle it could impose a penalty forbidding completely the exercise of that right—which it plainly may not do.

The lowering of tax exemptions for children after the first is meant to deter having more children. Of course, such a deterrence is a penalty.

Q

Does the graduated lowering of tax exemptions for children discriminate unfairly?

In commenting on a White House committee's suggestion that tax exemptions be lowered on children following the first, you said the lowering was a penalty.

I protest your short-sighted, circular reasoning.

Have we become so accustomed to receiving largess from Uncle Sam that we now consider ourselves deprived when it is no longer available? If my wife and I make the private decision to have more children, why should I expect other people (taxpayers) to help me pay for them?

A

The tax exemption under discussion is not "largess from Uncle Sam" even in a negative way. A person needs so much of this world's resources as an essential for staying alive. No government has a right to deprive him of this subsistence or any part of it. Hence a tax exemption on basic subsistence belongs by natural right to the individual and is no governmental gift.

Ordinarily the exemption should be equal for everyone unless some people as a class, like dependent children, have less expenses and therefore may have less of an exemption. Discriminating among dependent children, though, solely on the aspect of their chronological order in the family is patently unfair. The basic living requirements of 14-, 15-, and 16-year-old brothers certainly differ little. They all have the same insatiable appetite.

Q

May government limit the procreation of children with major deficiencies?

Yale geneticist Dr. Y. Edward Hsia raised this question at the 139th meeting of the American Association for the Advancement of Science, the world's largest scientific organization:

"If a family has a major risk of bearing children with major deficiencies, it is not only a tragedy for the individual and the family, but society may have to shoulder a major share of the medical and social cost of caring for such an individual.

"If such a family should choose to ignore the risk and continue to procreate, the cost to society will be multiplied by the birth of each affected individual.

"In such a situation, can society take upon itself the right to limit the number of children such a family might bear?"

Hsia answered in the affirmative. Would you?

A

The right of deciding about marriage and having children, whether deformed or not, belongs to the individual. It is given by nature. No ruler nor majority vote may deprive him of it.

Of course, married couples facing a decision about having children are bound by the moral laws. They must, for example, be reasonably able to meet the responsibilities of parenthood or have some justifying reason for risking parenthood with less than the ordinary, reasonable hope of being able to fulfill their obligations. But no one knows better than they the personal factors involved in the decision. To deny them the freedom to make that decision affecting their persons abuses their dignity as humans.

Q

May a woman be sterilized for the sake of her career?

Don't young people who are out for a career and feel they can't successfully have a career and children too or are simply opposed to having children of their own have a right to be sterilized?

A

People have no right to lop off a hand or to undergo any mutilation unless it is a necessary and the relatively least harmful means of preserving the health of a more important part of the body. But sterilization for the purpose stated in your question is not a necessary means. The young people have the capability, through the use of free-will, of avoiding sexual intercourse and thereby not having children. They are not free therefore to resort to mutilation to accomplish what they can through harmless means.

Furthermore, sterilization for a contraceptive purpose usurps God's dominion over human life. People have direct dominion over lesser forms of life but not over human life. There they must conform to the divine rule which in the physiology of generation is expressed through nature. As a result, they may not obstruct the natural consequences of coitus.

Q

Should a husband uproot a family for a better job?

I've worked for an important company for nearly 20 years. Business is not the best now and the company has ordered me to take a job 400 miles away or forget working for the company—which means giving up the pension and other securities I've built up during the years. My question is: Should I move and keep my security or uproot my family from friends and surroundings they love? (The older children refuse to move.)

A

In general, you ought to consider the friends and the roots which your family has put into the community of more importance than the financial security offered by a business firm. Enjoying the companionship of friends and being part of the community constitute more of living than what money can buy. Only the unwise would trade friends for luxuries.

However, if the financial security offered by the company is necessary for the basics of life and you cannot find work elsewhere, then apparently you would have no choice: you would have to move.

Q

Must a husband forgive and forget his wife's infidelity?

My wife was getting a massage and the masseur made love to her. They went all the way. She said it just happened and she's sorry.

What does a husband do in a case like that? Forgive and forget?

A

You have a right to put your unfaithful wife out into the cold. Whether you should exercise that right or forgive and forget, depends upon circumstances—the extent of your wife's guilt, the barrier which the fault sets up between the two of you, the consequences to others and especially to the children, and so forth. Ordinarily, you would do better by forgiving.

Q

May a husband escape the Iron Curtain and leave his family behind?

Every once in a while a case will get into print telling how a person had fled an Iron Curtain country and left his family behind.

Those abandoned are seldom given permission to leave.

In those circumstances, is it morally right for the person to leave just to save himself?

A

The man has a right to escape the Iron Curtain. In doing so he is not acting unjustly towards his wife and children by leaving them. The injustice is on the part of the jailers for not allowing the family to act freely and follow him.

Similarly, a free man is not bound to join his family behind the Iron Curtain.

Q

May an 83-year-old mother be sent to a nursing home rather than burden the family with her?

Is there anything immoral about sending my 83-year-old mother to a nursing home rather than burdening my family with her. My wife says we ought to keep her with us.

A

Honoring your mother in her present situation means seeing that she gets tender, loving care. Ordinarily a home with the family, not an impersonal nursing home with its loneliness, provides the care she needs in her old age. Of course, caring for her will cause some inconvenience but maybe not nearly as much as you caused her when you were young.

In general, only when mother is truly beyond the capability of the family to care for her at home, should she be released to a nursing home.

Q

Does the age at which one has unmarried sex make an essential, moral difference?

I'm going on 15 now and my step-father is 41. Well, a couple months back he found out I had gone to bed with my girl friend. And he really blew his stack.

I asked him how come it was O.K. for him and mom to sleep together before they were married.

He said they were older and that it was different.

That's the only answer he's given me and he won't let me bring up the subject anymore; he just glares.

I still don't see how age makes that much difference. I figure we're either both right or both wrong.

A

You were both wrong. But your step-father is at least now acting correctly in correcting you.

Q

Should we live with and accept homosexuality?

A physician, Dr. Howard J. Brown, admitted publicly before a group of 600 doctors at a meeting in New Jersey on human sexuality that he has been a homosexual for 30 years. He urged the doctors to help patients accept and live with rather than conceal homosexuality, "to help free them from the fear and agony of secrecy," since homosexuality is usually not a treatable abnormality. He received sustained applause.

Contrary to the usual moralistic fumings, isn't the doctor correct?

A

The fact that homosexual activities, bestiality, and sexual abuse of children may not, any more than theft and murder, be prevented by psychotherapy is no reason for claiming they are moral or allowable in the community. Homosexuality is a perversion of nature, not as degrading as bestiality or child abuse but shameful enough that it should be suppressed and by no means paraded as acceptable activity.

The physicians who applauded Dr. Brown's stand are poor moralists. As physicians they help to heal bodies, but as moralists they are in danger of directing humans to unhappiness and thereby rather negating the good they did in the first place—like a mechanic expertly repairing a car but then giving directions which lead the driver over a cliff.

Q

Is thinking about sex wrong?

I read somewhere that thinking about sex is the same as adultery. I thought it was normal for teenagers (I'm one) to think about what it would be like.

A

People naturally will think about sex. There is nothing immoral about the mere thinking. Immorality consists in willing to do evil—to do what is morally forbidden. (Actually carrying out the evil desire adds to the immorality.) So a person can be morally a murderer, adulterer, robber even though he may not have the opportunity to put his evil desires into practice. It was in that sense that Christ spoke of a man being an adulterer for lusting after a woman in his heart.

In order to avoid immoral desires, it may be necessary sometimes to avoid even thinking of the forbidden matter lest the thinking will arouse a natural desire that will prove overpowering. For that reason it is good for unmarried persons, for whom sex is forbidden, to keep their minds occupied with other things.

Q

Is there really a difference between a wife and a prostitute?

Dr. B. Appelbaum, a clinical psychologist from Berkeley, California, says there's no real difference between a wife and a prostitute. He says that both play up the male ego. One does it for money, the other for security.

I feel he's wrong, but I can't explain it.

A

The prostitute has no moral right to sexual intercourse with her client. The wife, though, not only has a right but normally a duty to lie with her husband.

Furthermore, in a perfect marital relationship the wife gratifies her husband out of love that seeks union and the pleasure of the beloved, not out of a selfish motive of security.

Q

Are sex therapy organizations permissible?

A sex therapy organization uses women as sex trainers of men who are total strangers. Although the women have sexual intercourse with the patients and are paid $50 for a two hour period, they are not considered prostitutes.

Does the fact that therapy is involved change things that much?

A

Robbing a store in order to give to charity is still robbery and an evil. So too a therapeutic purpose does not change the nature of prostitution. The women in the organization are prostitutes.

Q

How can having an illegitimate baby be wrong when it brings so much happiness?

A friend of mine who at 30 felt her chances of marriage were slim decided not to wait longer but got herself pregnant and had a baby so she could have someone to live for. She put no strings on the boy's father. Both baby and mother are doing just fine.

I'm sure you'll say that what she did was immoral, but I don't see why. She's happy, the baby's happy.

A

Your friend has the normal yearnings of a woman. Fulfilling them would naturally bring her a certain satisfaction.

A child, though, has a right to the loving care of both parents. But since a single person cannot by herself meet that responsibility of parenthood, she is not free to beget a child. Nor, since she is single, is she free even to have sex.

Q

Is there anything morally good about commune living?

Is there anything to be said for communal family living as practiced by the hippie type?

A

If the hippie type keeps within the rules of morality, communal living could be an agreeable experience at least for a time. People could find the companionship very pleasant; and from a lack of great concern about material things and from the spirit of generosity demanded of them they could fall heir to a lightheartedness, a serenity and sense of brotherhood typical of novice monks.

As time passes, differences in human nature would come to the front. Some members of the commune would shirk their duties. Arguments would arise over the use of common possessions. Desire for security and advantages over and above what the commune offers would prompt separations. The natural tendency for independence would cause others to drop out. In general, a commune cannot long exist except when its members are highly motivated like a religious community; nature is against it.

Chapter 8

Fair and Unfair

Discrimination

Q

Is a public school's "affirmative action" policy of admitting minority students ahead of better qualified non-minority students fair?

The University of Washington Law School has an "affirmative action" policy of admitting minority students even though non-minority students seeking admission have better qualifications. The school claims it has an overriding interest in promoting integration in public education. A young man, a non-minority member, while suing the school for not admitting him said the school has no right to put up any race as a privileged class and deny him his rights simply because he is not of that race.

The Anti-Defamation League of B'Nai B'rith argued for the plaintiff and said the school's policy is morally wrong. The Supreme Court sidestepped the issue.

Which side are you on?

A

The University of Washington Law School is discriminating against non-minority citizens. The fact is obvious. The question is: May a public school so discriminate?

A public school seems to have a right to discriminate—to experiment with filling its classes with a fixed quota of people from various races or even to require complete segregation—in order, say, to waylay racial tension due imminently to bring great harm unless solved. It is merely allowing the lesser of two evils. But it does not seem to have the right ordinarily to use discrimination, in what should be fair competition, as a means of improving the status of the less qualified. By doing so it causes the person discriminated against considerable and certain harm, whereas it does the person favored only a dubious good. In other words, it seems to be doing more harm than good.

Trying to help the poor and ignorant through such discrimination stifles loyalty towards the community and ambition towards productiveness in those who give the best promise of being the most productive citizens. The entire country, rich and poor alike, normally is best served by admitting first to education people like Albert Einstein and George Washington Carver than people much less qualified. The country ought to reward achievement and thereby encourage ambition. The opposite, rewarding under-achievement, kills ambition, encourages idleness, and fosters a never ending slide downward leading to an equality of poverty.

The poor and ignorant can best be helped by opening the same opportunities to them for self-improvement as are open to all people. Sometimes, too, they may require "missionary" help to bring them to the point where they can and want to take advantage of, at least, basic opportunities. But in actual competition it seems they should normally be shown no favoritism.

Q

May Yellow Cab refuse to hire drivers with long hair?

In justice do courts have the right to tell the Yellow Cab Company to hire drivers with long hair?

A

The owner, in this case the Yellow Cab Company, has the responsibility of caring for his business. The courts do not. Consequently the owner, not the courts, has the right to choose the employees who he thinks will help the business and to direct them in matters related to the business, such as job apportionment, dress, grooming, deportment, record keeping, and so forth.

The employees, on their part, by accepting employment agree to follow the owner's directives concerning his business. They freely limit their own choice in the matter. Hence, they are not being wronged when they are required to wear a uniform, have their hair groomed to suit the boss's concept of what is best for the business, to be courteous always, and so on—provided nothing required is immoral.

Q

May the telephone company discriminate and not hire homosexuals?

Homosexuals bitterly criticized the Pacific Telephone Company for having a policy of not hiring known homosexuals. They said the policy is an unwarranted intrusion into private sexuality, forcing them to lead "double lives"—to conceal their homosexuality—if they want jobs with the phone company.

As much as I dislike homosexuals, aren't they correct in this instance?

A

The phone company, as the one responsible for the business, has a right to discriminate regarding the character of its employees, to be intolerant of character traits that grate on customers or hurt the spirit of friendship and cooperation which should exist among fellow employees. It recognizes, praise be, that the normal person reacts towards faggots somewhat as he does towards maggots.

Homosexuals have no claim to a prior right. They have no inherent right to be hired by the phone company, much less at their own bidding and under their own terms.

Q

May a landlord rent to single men only?

A landlord in Redwood City, California, was sued by a woman charging him with "arbitrary discrimination on the basis of sex." (Sex bias is against the law in California.) She said he rents to single men but not to women.

I'm a landlord and I sympathize with the guy in Redwood City. I think he should be able to keep his rental for all men or all women if he wants.

What's your stand?

A

Morally, proprietorship does not give the landlord a right to turn people in dire straits away from sharing in his abundance. Thus, if there were an acute housing shortage so that a woman would be without adequate shelter unless he took her in, he would be obliged to do so. Otherwise, proprietorship gives him the right to do what he thinks best for developing his property. And for a thousand and one reasons he could well think it best to have only men tenants. Hence, ordinarily he has a right to exclude women.

Unless government can prove that a housing shortage or some other community need is so acute that rentals must be on a rather first come, first served basis, anything like a sex bias law usurps, in my judgment, the right of proprietorship and therefore is unjust and invalid.

Furthermore, requiring or banning motives for an action is beyond the competency of law. A law, for instance, can require that a young man join the army and fight for his country, but it cannot require him to do so out of a motive of patriotism. So too it seems that forbidding a citizen from not renting from a motive of sex, race or religious bias is beyond the competency of law and is therefore invalid. Short of self-confession, motives cannot be known with the certitude necessary for conviction.

Q

Should every sizeable, disadvantaged group be represented on every public board and commission?

In a democratic society shouldn't every sizeable, disadvantaged group be represented on every public board and commission? I think it's about time Filipinos get what's theirs.

A

A democratic, pluralistic society has a duty to lessen as far as possible divisiveness among her people. She seeks to weld a unity that makes for a strong, vital community. The unity she strives for is a political one and quite compatible with a diversity of national origins, cultures, religions and the like. She counts the latter differences as nothing in the political sphere but looks only at the ability of the citizen to share in the responsibility of governing—at his intelligence, knowledge of the issues facing the government, and sense of duty towards the country.

Thus, she may not set up one group as worthy of special political muscle because of being Filipino, Buddhist, an association of druggists, female, within the age of 30-35, or whatever. To do so would be divisive—as though belonging to the particular group, and not intelligence, civic knowledge and patriotism, gave a person more reason to run the government than anyone else. She must allow, however, any such group to lobby to protect its special interests.

If the above were not true and the community free to proportion out her governing seats to every cultural, racial, etc. group, she would slip into chaotic anarchy in her attempt to satisfy the myriads of divergent groups which rightly would be seeking representation.

Chapter 9

News Media and

Its Rights

Q

What right of secrecy have newsmen?

According to the Gallup poll the majority of Americans believe a newspaper reporter should not be required by courts or anyone to reveal confidential information and news sources. They feel the newsman needs confidentiality to bring wrong doing to light. Yet some people think the prosecutor should have a right to get at the newsman's sources so criminals can be punished.

What's your feeling on the matter?

A

Everyone, not merely a newsman, is obliged to keep legitimate committed secrets. Everyone, including the combined session of both houses of Congress and the U.S. Supreme Court, must respect the obligation. Of course, recognizing the obligation in specific instances is not always easy. Or in general instances, as witness some of the 20 or more bills before a subcommittee of the House Judiciary Committee.

None of the bills, by the way, seem to have a complete grasp of the nature of secrecy as it pertains to newsmen. The closest appears to be Rep. Edward Koch's H.R. 837.

Now, what is a committed secret? It is information committed only after a promise of secrecy—a promise which is presupposed in certain professions requiring confidences. Not all information, though, is legitimate matter for secrecy; a promise may be made but the matter itself can preclude secrecy.

Legitimate matter of newsmen's secrecy falls under two categories: (1) information given in confidence that does not pertain to future unjust action, like a plot for murder, or that does not inflict a grave misfortune on the newsman himself unless he expressly agreed to allow it; (2) identity of the confidential source except when the act of informing was in itself a violation of rightfully imposed secrecy or when the source uses secrecy to violate justice with impunity, say, through libel.

Secrecy is meant to effect good, not evil. It is not meant to facilitate crime or to be used as an excuse to omit preventing crime. Hence, no newsman ordinarily has a right to withhold information when revealing it would probably assure the prevention of unjust harm; in fact, he usually has a positive duty to reveal it. The same, too, can be said about revealing the identity of sources: the newsman is free of any bond of secrecy when secrecy would permit the source to do unjust harm, like carry out a murder or leak secrets of a grand jury. And it should be presupposed that he would not promise to keep a matter secret which will cause his own self a grave misfortune.

But ought confidential information about past crimes be kept secret when the community is trying to teach people a lesson by punishing the culprits? Ordinarily the information must be kept secret because the definite, immediate good of being able to have confidences outweighs the remote, indefinite good resulting from the wheels of justice punishing any particular law-violator.

The very fact that it is a newsman who sees and hears something does not of itself place the matter under a bond of secrecy. There must be at least an implied promise of confidentiality. Thus the newsman who witnesses a murder while strolling home from work or observes a riot even as a matter of assignment may ordinarily be called to testify.

Of course, the newsman is always free to reveal his confidential information or source whenever the source releases him.

Two final notations:

Since a newsman is in a special position of trust regarding confidences, he should rather readily be excused from testifying lest people mistakenly be scandalized and come to distrust him.

Although he often witnesses events which later involve court action, he should not be treated as an arm of the police. When his help is needed often and burdensomely, he ought to be recompensed.

Q

Do student newspapers have editorial freedom?

The student newspaper of Florida Atlantic University in Boca Raton irritated the university president who promptly fired the editor and the two assistant editors. The three students went to a federal court and got this favorable ruling from U. S. District Judge Joe Eaton: The university administration can choose to have no campus newspaper, publish a newsletter, or give the students a free hand to print what they like; if it chooses to have a student newspaper, "it cannot control the contents."

Does freedom of the press stretch that far?

A

Freedom of the press is not unlimited. It is limited by other rights—the right of people not to be unjustly maligned, the right of press owners to the administration of their property, and so on. Hence, if the school owns the newspaper, the student editors are bound to submit to the directive of the school which has the ultimate responsibility for seeing that the paper is used for good and not evil—and not against the goals of the university. Even if the students own the newspaper, they must respect the authority of the school administration over campus activity and therefore over the distribution of the paper on campus.

Q

Should reporters hide personal scandals of public figures?

Newsmen generally do not tell on a politician they find stinking drunk. His personal faults they keep private. But is this policy correct? Shouldn't the public know whether their elected representative is a drunk or a man who can be trusted to do a good job?

A

Newsmen, as well as everyone else, have a duty not to blacken anyone's character unnecessarily. No one should tell of another's faults unless the good to be accomplished by telling outweighs the harm done the person's reputation. Thus, when someone sees another drinking rather heavily and habitually, he may tell the latter's wife or friend so that the man can be prevented from becoming an alcoholic or can get help if he is one. Likewise, newsmen may inform the public about a politician's drinking habits when, say, the habits so interfere with the effectiveness of his service to the people that the resulting harm outweighs the harm to the man's reputation.

Q

Does the press have the right to grand jury secret information that is beneficial to the public?

Columnist Jack Anderson somehow got and published secret testimony given the grand jury investigating the Watergate affair. He said it is the constitutional right of the free press to publish information that is beneficial to the public. He swore he'd never reveal who told him the secrets.

But Chief Judge John J. Sirica wanted to find out where the leak was. He said the grand jury investigations "are secret and must remain so" to protect the innocent and "encourage free disclosure by persons who have information with respect to possible commission of crimes."

Who's correct?

A

One right can be limited by another. The right of the free press to gather and publish information is limited by people's right of privacy, by a government's right to secrecy in certain matters, and so forth. Of course, everything the press publishes should be beneficial to the public or it should not be published. It seems, therefore, that Jack Anderson exaggerated the right of the press.

Also, leaking the grand jury secret information was an illegal act which he witnessed. Even though he had promised to keep the identity of the law-violator secret, he was not bound to do so since his confidentiality was being used for evil, for breaching the right of confidentiality which the grand jury had. In fact, he was bound to reveal the source when asked by legitimate authority.

Q

Does the "fairness doctrine" of the Federal Communications Commission muzzle free speech?

Radio and television broadcasters' licenses must be renewed every three years by the Federal Communications Commission, which has begun to put pressure on the station licensees to balance the news and rid themselves of consistent bias or face the possibility that their licenses will not be renewed.

Isn't the pressure unfair? Isn't it a form of muzzling free speech?

A

Apparently, only a specific number of stations can presently be accommodated on the air-waves of a given area. Hence broadcasters enjoy a certain monopoly which ought to be strictly supervised by the community lest it be used against the common good. It is only reasonable, therefore, that the government demands a balance of the news and an absence of editorial bias. If all major stations took the same, certain bias and made a determined effort to have their view prevail throughout the country, the people could hardly resist the brainwashing. (Reportedly, the stations did just that in Sweden and with the expected results.)

What constitutes proper balance ought to be decided by an impartial group of citizens, not by partisaned government administrators or politicians.

Q

Should reporters with state capitol press credentials lose them if they become candidates for state offices?

Should reporters with state capitol press credentials giv-
ing them access to the senate and assembly floors and an
office in the building lose the credentials if they become
candidates for a state office? After an overwhelming vote
in favor of the restriction reporters in Sacramento made
the proposal to the Joint Rules Committee of the legisla-
ture.

I thought it was an open and shut case because of the bias
the candidate-reporter would be expected to have. But the
Committee turned down the proposal and a legislator said
the proposal was an infringement of the constitutional
right of freedom of the press.

How do you see it?

A

The legislator's reasoning against the proposal seems very
wide of the mark. Necessity allows only a limited number
of capitol press credentials and it is only fair that the most
deserving get them—which ordinarily eliminates reporters
with a likely conflict of interest. What is done through necessity cannot be an unjust infringement of a constitutional right.

Q

**Ought newspapers to give equal space for replies to
their criticisms of politicians?**

Florida has a little used state law that requires newspa-
pers to give equal space and importance to a reply by a polit-
ical candidate they might have "assailed." The Miami Her-
ald is now being sued for not having complied with the law.

Does the law violate the right of a free press as the Herald
claims?

A

People have a right to express their judgments through newspapers, magazines, books, pamphlets and other printed forms. It is simply part of their natural right of free speech. The right allows them to speak freely when and if they choose—as long as they cause no unjust harm—and through whatever media they can manage on their own; it does not entitle them to have the media put gratuitously at their disposal. Thus, if a person lacks the speaking ability or money to have his voice heard on a par with an opponent, by no means is the opponent obliged to help him reach an equality. Furthermore, any law which would try to force that equality would be doing the opponent an injustice for it would be stifling his freedom of speech by making him bear the cost of his opposition's opportunity for refutation. People would not be inclined to speak up and have their views known and do their part in trading ideas if they had to pay for their opposition.

A certain "equal time" seemingly ought to be given on television and radio under some circumstances. But that is because of the quasi-monopoly which the electronic media enjoy. Newspapers, however, can multiply as fast as there are capital and people interested in setting them up.

Q

Does the "right of freedom of the press" mean the right of free access to the media?

There's a growing demand for the government to force newspapers to give private individuals equal space for replies. The National News Council regards the push for equal time as an attempt to interpret the First Amendment as saying that the public has a right to access to the media.

Does the public have that right?

A

Morally, the First Amendment should mean that man is free to speak out in any way he can as long as he does unjust harm to no one. Man has a right to such freedom. He has a right to have his message spread as widely as his ability and resources can muster—to have it printed, aired over radio and television, carried on banners by dirigibles—as long as he does no one unjust harm. Ordinarily, though, he would be doing unjust harm if he seized control over someone else's resources in order to spread his own ideas.

If it were true that everyone could use anything at any time he felt a need for it even though it belonged to someone else, ownership would be an empty title and responsibility, which is needed for the proper care of things, would be completely lacking.

Q

Should "help-wanted" ads with sex preference be permitted?

Should newspapers be compelled to reclassify their "help-wanted" ads so that no sex preference is shown? When an employer wants a doorman or a busboy or a barmaid, shouldn't he be free to advertise for what he wants?

A

An employer, by the fact of his responsibility for the proper administration of his property, normally has a duty to discriminate in choosing employees. He has the responsibility for picking fellow-workers who will help the business, people who are industrious, intelligent, capable of doing the tasks assigned—whether carrying bricks or dealing sweetly and patiently with clients—and who contribute to the general team atmosphere, and so on. Under ordinary circumstances he has a basic moral right to pick a male, 60-year-old, left-handed Chinese if he thinks those qualifications are best for his business; and since he has that right, he has a right to advertise for the type of help he wants.

The press in the matter is merely his servant.

Q

Must the press obey unjust court orders?

Two reporters wrote accounts of a public civil rights hearing in a Baton Rouge, La., federal district court despite the fact that the court had ordered a prohibition against such accounts. The reporters were promptly held in contempt. Later, the court's ban against the news was declared illegal. But there's a wrangle as to whether or not the reporters should be allowed to go free. The Justice Department thinks they shouldn't be freed. What's your thought?

A

Illegal or unjust laws must be obeyed when disobedience would cause more harm than good.

How important to the community was the news of the civil rights trial? Would the news impair the trial in any way? Was the over-all good of telling the news worth the disobedience to the court and the bad example it gave of disrespect for authority? These are some of the questions that have to be answered before a good judgment could be made on whether the two reporters' disobedience was justified.

Courts are run by humans who can err. Corrections as far as possible must be made in an orderly, non-disruptive fashion otherwise judicial authority breaks down and causes man a harm immensely greater than that of not getting the news from a thousand civil rights trials.

Q

Is advocacy journalism in the news media proper?

I've heard so much about the unfairness of the news media. Do you think it's unfair?

A

Since the media is staffed by humans, some unfairness must be expected. The usual human failings—lethargy, thoughtlessness, anxiousness to be dramatic or to please the boss—can account for much unfairness. A reporter may not bother to check out the truth of a rumor that he uses, or he may intimate for dramatic effect on television, say, that the strike of the airline ticket agents will shut down all plane traffic whereas he knows the airline management will fill in for the ticket agents and keep all traffic going at normal pace. Such failings and consequent unfairness must be expected as part of living among humans.

Unfortunately, too, many people in the news media today do not seem satisfied with the job of simply presenting straight, objective news and letting us interpret the facts for ourselves; they evidently want something more meaningful to do so they have taken to interpreting the facts for us. Theirs is known as advocacy journalism. Here is an example:

Recently the New York Times Service sent out under the guise of straight news a report about Chile cracking down on cocaine traffic destined for the United States. The facts by themselves would have brought praise to the Chilean rulers. But the *Times* writer did not let the facts stand by themselves. He supplied gratuitously his own preconceived notion of the motive for the crackdown and wove in also his personal belief in the innocence of Allende's Marxist followers whom the rulers oppose. By so doing he changed the complexion of the rulers' action from a good to a nearly contemptuous, self-serving thing.

Such reporting is certainly unfair; it is anything but straight.

Q

May business editors tout stocks to their personal advantage?

The business editor of a newspaper has a golden opportunity to buy a stock when it's low, glamorize it in his column and, when the price goes up, sell. He can easily take advantage of the public.

Can you suggest some ethical guidelines for the business editors?

A

The job of the business editor is to help his readers to a better grasp of reality in the world of finances. It is not to play a "confidence" game on them to line his pockets. He should be able, though, to take his own advice.

As a check on his honesty, the newspaper may oblige him to submit periodically a complete financial accounting.

Chapter 10
Nudity and Obscenity

Q

Should national distributors of magazines be obliged to contend with thousands of obscenity standards?

The U.S. Supreme Court decided that local juries should be the judge of obscenity. But isn't that unfair to the national distributor of magazines and films who has no way of contending with thousands of standards? Shouldn't the Supreme Court be more explicit in defining obscenity?

A

Obscenity could be defined as that which offends the virtuously modest and arouses lewd desires in the not-so-virtuous. It is subjective inasmuch as it affects each person according to his disposition—maturity, education, extent of virtue, etc.—and hence no two people in exactly the same way. Yet it is objective inasmuch as it can affect similarly entire groups of people, as pornographers well know, because of their general sameness of disposition.

Because of this objective element, pornography can be

117

recognized and outlawed. Yet since the subjective aspect plays such a prominent part, determining and outlawing what is obscene ought to be done primarily by local communities who best know the disposition of their own citizens. After all, communities can differ culturally and in their sense of modesty. What will offend one and be an occasion leading her to evil may be absolutely inoffensive to another. At the same time each community has a duty to protect herself and may not ordinarily be forced into lowering her standards to her harm. The Amish community, for instance, should not be subjected to the scandal that would come from being forced into accepting the standards of a cosmopolitan "sin" city.

Higher governments can be less strict as long as the lower government can be as strict as it thinks necessary to protect its people.

Seemingly, the national distributor of possibly pornographic material ought not to be prosecuted for an offense against local obscenity laws when his product is legal elsewhere in the nation; but the local seller should be. The trouble the national distributor is put to in finding outlets for his product because of the lack of uniformity in law does him no injustice. He has no right to require people to buy his product.

Q

Doesn't censorship break with a free society which realizes that what is good for one man may be bad for another?

Along with the Supreme Court you've favored each community having its own power of censorship over smut. But how do you answer someone like Justice William O. Douglas who says that censorship breaks with the traditions of a free society which realizes that what's bad for one person may be good for another?

A

Every law is a form of censorship. It says the citizen is not free to do whatever he pleases about the matter involved in the law but must act in such-and-such a manner.

Laws, of course, are enacted to meet the general run of circumstances affecting the common good; and most of them must allow for exemptions due to changes in circumstances.

Laws against pornography are no different. They forbid an activity harmful to the citizens in general.

Q

Should swimmers be allowed to swim nude in Olympic competition?

Some Olympic swimmers find they can swim faster naked than in a bathing suit. Morally can they be allowed to compete nude? They would probably lower the records.

A

Nudity in itself is not immoral. Circumstances make it so. Nudity, for example, during a medical examination is one thing; while alone in the house with a date is quite another. Only when the circumstances are such that nakedness incites to unchastity, is it immoral.

Are the circumstances such that swimmers can morally be allowed to compete nude in the Olympics? In my judgment, virtuous parents with lots of children would probably not be affected adversely by the sight of naked young men and women. The same most likely could be said of doctors and nurses as well as "swingers" accustomed to seeing people naked. Otherwise, I suspect, there would be a lot of ogling deleterious to chastity.

Q

Is communal bathing allowable?

What do you think of communal bathing where friends of the neighborhood, men and women, all get in the same big hot tub together naked? Being nude doesn't seem to embarrass them.

A

When because of circumstances nudity incites to immoral desire or action, it is immoral.

Would communal bathing, at least in the Western world that we know, ordinarily incite to immoral desires or actions? I think so. Of course, practitioners of indiscriminate "free-love" may be satiated enough sexually that mere nudity constitutes little or no immediate stimulus, yet even so I suspect the nudity would encourage them to remain sexually uninhibited and would therefore be immoral on that score.

Q

Are nudist camps permissible?

What's your opinion of nudist camps?

A

Public nudity normally is a proximate occasion of moral evil. No one may place himself unnecessarily in such an occasion.

Furthermore, clothes seem to be adornments that belong to civilization. They inspire respect and add a beauty that brings delight. Even animals are sometimes dressed. But a trend towards nudism is a trend away from civilization and the virtues which civilization cultivates. Hence nudists seem to be following a retrogressive course towards savagery.

Q

How can Nevada allow prostitution and yet ban X-rated movies?

Storey County in Nevada legalized prostitution yet planned to ban topless performances and X-rated movies and such sex-related activities which might "excite or stimulate prurient interests."

Isn't that a contradiction in moral principles—camel-swallowing but gnat-straining?

A

Morally, prostitution can be legalized in order to avoid a greater evil. For instance, the possibility of virtuous women being raped could be so great and imminent that allowing brothels could be the only practical answer; or, venereal disease could be so rampant that for health reasons prostitution would have to be legalized so infections could be controlled. In such cases the community is simply trying to lessen the evil that already exists.

But in banning topless performances and X-rated movies and other such sex-related activities the community is trying to prevent evil from coming into existence and to eliminate at the roots a cause of prostitution.

Chapter 11

Man and the State

Q

May former felons be barred from voting?

Does a state have a moral right to deny former felons the right to vote? After a man has paid his debt to society, shouldn't he have all rights like anyone else?

A

Voting is a way of participating in the rule of a community. Not everyone should be allowed to rule. Ruling requires knowledge of the issues facing the community, prudence in choosing the right course of action under the existing circumstances, and love for the community so that what is done is done for the good of the community. As general groups, the young, the illiterate, and the insane lack the first two requirements; felons, the third. Normally, they should not be allowed to vote.

The mere fact that a felon completes his punishment is no indication he has changed inwardly and will not wilfully harm the community again. Unless there is good evidence of a change for the better, it seems he should be held suspect and the benefit of the doubt be given the safety of the community. Moreover, taking away his voting franchise can reasonably be part of his punishment.

Q

May courts ever be disobeyed?

When Gerald Ford was the Vice Presidential nominee, he was asked in a committee hearing whether he would ever disobey a court ruling. The obvious allusion was to President Nixon and the doubt he had raised about obeying a court order. Ford quickly responded in the negative and pleased his questioners.

Was Ford correct? Couldn't there be times when the court could be wrong and shouldn't be obeyed?

A

If the court commands an unjust action, it must not be obeyed. For instance, it could rule that a newspaper man or a government administrator has to reveal what is truly a professional secret; under such circumstances the court must not be obeyed. Likewise, it could overstep its rightful jurisdiction and attempt, say, to take over the affairs of the executive branch; but it ought not to be obeyed since obedience would be a betrayal of the executive duties according to the constitution.

The person disobeying, of course, may have to suffer for the sake of justice or the constitution.

Q

Is health care a basic right like life, liberty and happiness?

If health care is a basic right like life, liberty and the pursuit of happiness, doesn't that mean the government is morally bound to institute some form of national health insurance?

A

We are bound to take ordinary care of our health and the health of those under our charge. We have a right, therefore, to the means of fulfilling our duty. The right, though, like the right to food and shelter, is not unconditional. Normally we have to earn our health care just as we do our food and shelter. We cannot be drones and expect others to work for our upkeep.

Government is bound, in general, to promote our self-reliance so that we stand on our own feet and do as much as we can for ourselves. For self-reliance means freedom, and government should constantly be striving to promote freedom. It should be a facilitator, clearing away obstacles and setting up circumstances in which we can easily perform our duties of earning enough to eat, a place to sleep, an education for our children, reasonable health care and so forth. Ordinarily, only in cases of necessity should government actually step in and do for us.

It seems, therefore, that government ought to avoid as far as possible the paternalism of socialized medicine and seek instead to open up private opportunities for everyone willing to make a reasonable effort to have good health care.

Q

Is National Health Insurance a good thing?

Is there a moral angle to National Health Insurance? NHI is on its way, no one denies that; but could we be making a mistake?

A

The use of the world's goods belongs in common to all people. Nevertheless, the ownership of the goods must, in general, be private because only through the responsibility which proprietorship brings will the world's resources be preserved and cultivated sufficiently. As a consequence the laborer must own the fruit of his labor and as owner have the first claim to its use.

Only from the owner's abundance does someone else have, under certain conditions, a claim to use what the owner possesses. The owner, on his part, is obliged out of his abundance to help the man in great need; but he is obliged not to support indolence where people can but will not help themselves. Hence, in justice a national health insurance plan may not—unless there is a compensating good involved—force citizens to pay for unnecessary or extraordinary services for themselves or others, or for services for people who could but will not help themselves.

Are there national health schemes which avoid the injustices mentioned above and the paternalism referred to in the previous answer or possess compensating goods? Not to my knowledge. They seem to be no more than variations on the socialized medicine of Britain where great disillusionment has set in and people are turning in droves to private health care for the quality which proprietorship responsibility brings.

Q

Ought a free world power return hijackers seeking to escape tyranny?

While commenting on anti-hijacking pacts you once said that people should not be prevented from hijacking planes, boats or whatever in order to escape tyranny. In light of that what do you think of the latest United States agreement with Cuba calling for a return of hijackers except when the hijackers are seeking political refuge in the United States and arrive without using force?

A

Hijacking without using force, like squaring a circle, is a contradiction in terms. By the bit of doubletalk the pact simply bars hijacking as a means of escape.

All other means also seem to be blocked for the Cubans. They could hardly steal adequate transportation to freedom without using some force against guards or property. The only recourse apparently open to them under the agreement is floating to the U. S. A. on an old inner-tube—which they may be able to get without force.

People, though, have a right to escape tyranny and to use force against anyone who would prevent them. The United States for her part has a duty to help them as far as she can without suffering a disproportionate loss to herself. For her to omit this duty is immoral.

Q

Must a pluralistic society be neutral towards religion?

The Supreme Court recently prohibited states from helping church schools by giving parents tax credits as a form of tuition reimbursement. Justice Lewis F. Powell said that the government must remain "neutral" and avoid "advancing" religion, and that special tax benefits to parents with children in church schools would aid and advance those religious institutions.

Isn't Powell correct?

A

When citizens lose sight of the fact that their rights come from God and not from the state, they are ripe to be led into tyranny. In fact, a close relationship with God is a "must" for their well-being. Hence the community, pluralistic or not, must support religion in general. Her "neutrality" can only mean an impartiality in advancing the various religions; it cannot mean, as Justice Powell implies, a total abstention from all things religious because such an interpretation would actually be setting the community against religion and for atheism.

Q

Should handguns be outlawed?

A

As long as government does not sufficiently protect individuals from robbers, rapists and the like, individuals have a right and often a duty to protect themselves and their loved ones. Frequently a small, inexpensive handgun is the only practical means to that end.

Also, I think the possession of weapons by the general citizenry does much to cool the ambitions of a would-be tyrant. An armed populace is extremely hard to subdue. Of course, this assurance of freedom may cost lives (freedom usually does), but I reckon it worth the price.

Q

Is a country's suppression of free speech an internal, domestic matter?

One of the four principal aims of our participation in World War II was "freedom of speech—everywhere in the world." Yet today when dictators stop the free flow of information we allow them to get away with it because of our fear of involving ourselves in the "domestic affairs" of another country.

Is freedom of speech a purely "domestic affair" or do we have a right to interfere?

A

Freedom of speech is a natural right of man. Under ordinary circumstances no government can justly take it from him. If government does, he has a right to rebel and to be aided in the rebellion by his neighbors who have a duty to help him throw off the oppressor and even to do the entire job for him when he is unable to help himself.

In extraordinary situations a nation may have to curtail drastically the free flow of information. For instance, a country could be at war or her people so torn apart by dissention that they could not face up unitedly to necessary tasks for the common-good unless the source feeding the dissention were cut off. Free speech is meant to achieve good, not evil.

Q

Does freedom of speech allow "sex-talk" shows?

How do you reconcile freedom of speech and the desire some people have for getting rid of those "sex-talk" radio shows where the interviewer chats with unidentified women about the most intimate details of their sex lives?

A

Freedom of speech is not unlimited. No one is free to libel, tell secrets, encourage evil, or in any other way to hurt someone unjustly.

But giving adult, vividly detailed knowledge of sex to an immature person can be very harmful. Even swamping the reasonably mature person with phantasms and talk about sex can be a shove in the wrong direction. Hence, if "sex-talk" shows would normally be detrimental either to the immature or the mature segment of the audience, they ordinarily would have no right to be aired. There are other ways of giving out possibly needed sex information without causing harm because of their control over the type of audience and its general reaction.

Q

Does freedom of speech give the right to treat the country's flag contemptuously?

A Massachusetts law makes an offense of mutilating the American flag or otherwise treating it "contemptuously" like wearing it on the seat of one's pants. But the American Civil Liberties Union says forbidding such use of the flag would have a chilling effect on freedom of speech.

Who's correct?

A

Freedom of speech is not unlimited. Man has no right to use speech to do anyone unjust harm.

But treating contemptuously the flag of a basically just nation does more than merely show one's displeasure at this or that national policy which may be unfair or stupid; it also expresses forcibly a disrespect for rightful authority in general. Therefore, like a display of contempt in a courtroom for the presiding judge, the act ought to be liable to punishment lest the infection spread to the breakdown of authority and the disintegration of the community.

Q

Is there a moral angle to forming a metro government?

A lot of people say that the cities in our area ought to join together in one big government and do away with the waste, expense and inefficiency of segmented government. Others feel a metro government takes control away from the people.

How do you feel about it? Is there anything morally opposed to making one big city of the many?

A

According to the principle of subsidiarity people have a moral right to direct their own lives as far as their capacity to handle the situation will allow. Normally, therefore, the main government in their lives ought to be as close to home as possible. Other governments, state and federal, merely pick up the jobs which the local government cannot do for itself such as raising an army for the common defense, settling disputes between communities, regulating commerce among communities, states and foreign countries, and so forth.

The local community should jealously guard her autonomy and barter as little as possible away to cost-savings and efficiency (the sale's pitch of dictators), and prefer to put up with some extra expense and waste rather than give up freedom. Only through freedom can she, for instance, develop a colorful individuality and avoid the faceless look common to the regimented. Yet there can come a point when local government close to home is simply too costly and inefficient to be workable; consequently, it must cede to a higher, broader form of government.

Q

Do courts have a duty to articulate the community's "moral consensus"?

Not long ago columnist Anthony Lewis of the New York Times *said, "American society relies on the Supreme Court to deal with issues that politicians or the public itself have found too difficult." Then he gave segregation as an example and approvingly said: "Most Americans would surely have found it intolerable to continue for long after 1954 as a society in which blacks were legally excluded from many schools and jobs and restaurants. It took the Supreme Court to articulate that moral consensus and break the deadlock."*

How do members of the Court know when the country has reached a "moral consensus" on some issue?

A

In the United States a "moral consensus" or a majority agreement for government action is expressed through the ballot box and the people's legislative representatives. Until the people speak, judges can only guess like the rest of us at the "moral consensus."

In a government whose judicial, legislative and executive powers are separated, any court—including the Supreme Court—which would attempt to judge as Mr. Lewis claims the latter court does would be usurping legislative powers. Such a court would not be interpreting the law according to the mind of the lawgiver but would be altering the law and thereby legislating.

Q

What are the requisites for forming a new nation?

Morally, what determines whether a group of people can break away from the mother country and form a new nation? For example, does Bermuda with only 21 square miles and 55,000 people—about the size of a district in a big city—have a right to be an independent nation with representatives at the United Nations, etc.?

A

As far as possible people should be self-governing. But not always is national independence practical and for the good of the people. The group must be able to better the totality of its human conditions before it has a right to break away. In general, it must be relatively self-sufficient so that it can protect and support itself and thereby keep the whole community viable.

I suspect that Bermuda's 55,000 people would probably have major difficulties in qualifying. For one thing, they could only afford a few hundred police as security against internal and external enemies; seemingly they would be easy prey, say, for revolutionists who though few in number could catch the police by surprise and take over the country. On that point alone the people would seem to lack the potential for a stability of government necessary for peace and the promotion of their human conditions, and the rather imminent danger from the lack would seem to outweigh by far the curtailment of the people's freedom to direct themselves as a completely autonomous nation.

Q

May state employees get Good Friday off with pay?

A superior court judge in California ruled that state em-
ployees could not get time off on Good Friday with pay. The
ruling was in response to a young woman employee who
wanted Yom Kippur as the holiday instead of Good Friday.
He said: "Granting a paid period of worship on a Christian
holy day while denying the same benefit to those of another
religion serves to advance Christianity while not in like man-
ner advancing other faiths." His ruling also affects Christ-
mas.

All prejudices aside, isn't he correct?

A

Government has a duty to encourage religion among its
citizens and, hence, to honor religion. But the honor it pays
to any specific religion can only be in proportion to that
faith's importance in the community. Naturally, the major
faiths should receive the major honors. For example, when
the predominate number of citizens are Jewish, the government ordinarily should make Yom Kippur a holiday and Sat-
urday, instead of Sunday, the weekly day of rest. In the practical order a government cannot honor every religion with
absolute equality because either it would not be sufficiently
honoring the main faiths or it would never finish paying for
legal holidays, for sending representatives to new building
dedications, and the like.

Q

Should there be Community Legal Services?

The community legal services program is on the hot seat.
Complaints say that the poverty attorneys paid for by gov-
ernment should not be stressing class action directed at
elected officials and at reshaping laws and social institu-
tions, but that they should be putting all their attention on
individual services for indigent clients.

On the other hand, the poverty attorneys argue that class action helps many poor people at one time and is the most effective means of helping the poor.

Any answer?

A

The community runs her government through elected representatives who carry the responsibility of class action for the poor. It would be self-defeating for the community to finance an outside group to thwart the efforts of her chosen representatives. Seemingly, she would be doing just that if she allows her subsidized, poverty attorneys to attempt legislative changes, jail reforms, and the like.

In government there must be room for private citizens to contest laws and acts of the administration; but the onus of contesting must also be on the private citizens, not on the community.

Q

Which takes precedence, the community's or the individual's good?

I've read many comments by important people saying that they're happy the courts seem to be turning away from showing more concern for the individual than for society as a whole. Yet Justice Stanley Mosk of the California Supreme Court was recently reported as saying the Constitution takes the side of the individual over collective society, "guarding his security, his dignity, his claims to equal and fair treatment, against the ponderous demands of the collective state."

Where does morality stand?

A

Man is an amalgamation of an intellectual and material being.

As an intellectual being he is a person and superior to the community. The community is his servant, aiding him in the fulfillment of his person, safeguarding the freedoms he needs to achieve his goal as a person. So superior is he that he may not lessen his moral worth one iota to save all the communities in the world.

As a material being he is one among many, an individual, a part of the whole and, as such, subject to the community. On command, he must lay down his life in defense of the community.

The rights and duties of the community towards him and his towards the community are not contradictory in the least; in fact, they harmonize perfectly. The community has a duty to provide the freedom and opportunities necessary for his development as a person, and a right to require him to do his part in the common task of securing that freedom and those opportunities, even to the extent of laying down his life in her defense. (The patriotism she asks does not lessen his worth as a person but increases it.) On his part he has a right to have the community respect and work for him as a person, and a duty to sacrifice himself as an individual to keep the community strong and healthy. By sacrificing himself he gains as a person. On the other hand, by sacrificing herself for the individual the community loses, becomes weak and chaotic.

Hence, whenever the community stays within her legitimate sphere and respects the citizen as a person, then whatever is good for the community is not contrary to the good of the person and her good must be preferred to that of the individual.

Chapter 12

Student Power and

School Rights

Q

May loyalty oaths be required of teachers?

Is it right for a university to demand that teachers sign a loyalty oath before allowing them to teach?

The American Civil Liberties Union in San Francisco stated that the signing of the oath is "meaningless" and "demeaning" and against freedom of conscience.

A

Inasmuch as the community has a duty to foster her well-being and protect herself, she has a right to take the necessary steps for fulfilling that duty. Simple common sense demands that she require loyalty to her constitutional principles (an oath emphasizes the importance of the requirement) from people whom she places in position of influence. But university and college teachers have positions of great influence. They can do much to disrupt the community or to unify and strengthen her.

Teachers are free to hold privately the most perverse errors, yet they cannot be allowed to propagate them and harm the community. Freedom of conscience does not extend to action.

Q

May speakers be barred from campus?

Must a university be open to any speaker of enormous influence who wants to come on campus even though his ideas clash with those of the school?

A

The purpose of a university is to lead students to truth, encourage them to accept the good, and help them to appreciate beauty. Normally, anyone who would sabotage this purpose should not be given a campus podium; the university should not be working at cross purposes with itself.

Falsity can be presented but only to reveal truth more fully and relevantly. For instance, a speaker advocating the eventual suppression—through violence if necessary—of man's natural freedoms could be allowed on campus so that students can see that error truly exists and can come cleverly packaged; but the platform the speaker is given is one of an adversary, not of an advocate of truth.

Of course, in matters about which truth has not been decided there must be an open platform and robust discussion.

Q

Is the unequal funding of public schools through local property taxes unfair in a democratic society?

Isn't the unequal funding of public schools through local property taxes unfair in a democratic society? The rich

*neighborhoods are able to spend almost twice as much per
student as poor neighborhoods and they can do it with a
smaller tax rate. Isn't the system against the "equality of
opportunity" promised us by our government?*

A

"Equality of opportunity" which a democratic community
can and should provide is an equality of freedom from obstacles so that each member of the community is equally
unencumbered to pursue happiness according to his own
choosing. The community secures his person from the unjust aggression of internal and external enemies and pro-
motes in a positive way the general conditions under which
he can with relative ease meet his responsibilities in life.
"Equality of opportunity" does not mean that the community must supply what is lacking to make him equal in
every regard—financially, educationally, and so on—with
everyone else. Such an effort on the community's part would
run counter to her purpose of bringing as much freedom as
possible to her citizens because by taking over their responsibilities she would be making them dependent upon her
and would thereby be relieving them of their liberty. The
equality she offers is the sun and blue sky of freedom under
which the citizens can do for themselves without undue
interference.

The community rightly recognizes that parents have primary responsibility for the education of their children. She
can set a minimum standard of education, but she must allow the parents to do more for their children if they so
desire. Naturally, the rich will be able to do more, and without a big tax burden, than the poor.

The obligations of the community seem to be met quite
well by requiring people of a district to be in good part financially responsible for the schools in their district. Such a
system reasonably assures local parental control since the
person paying the piper normally calls the tunes; it also allows parents, who are willing and able, to do as much beyond the minimum as they want for their youngsters.

Q

Ought corporal punishment of students to be banned?

What's the moral answer to corporal punishment in schools? Shouldn't strapping be banned? I don't want my children told by a sadistic teacher, "Assume the position!" and be forced to bend over and grab their ankles and then be walloped.

A

The possibility of corporal punishment is almost a necessary inducement for children to stay on the proper road. Sweet reason often makes a small impression. But the possibility of physical pain or the loss of something which they cherish more than doing their own will in the disputed situation stands a good chance of bringing them into line.

Furthermore, corporal punishment is over with in a moment, painful but not harmful. The child gets his spanking and is then out into the milieu of his companions and normal life again, sad for a moment but often wiser for a lifetime.

What parents do, they can relegate to others. Thus, they can give the school the authority to corporally discipline their erring child.

Q

May school authorities search a student's locker without a search warrant?

Why do high school principals think they can search student lockers whenever they feel like it? Shouldn't they be made to get search warrants? Students have as much right not to be searched as anyone else.

A

High school students are normally under the jurisdiction of their parents. Parents need no search warrant to check their offspring's belongings when they suspect, say, that he is using drugs. Parents delegate that same authority to the school.

Q

Should everyone who can afford it have a college education?

My son is trying to convince me that not everyone who can afford it needs or should be given a college education. He, at 19, wants to be a sports' car mechanic! I want him to be a lawyer.

A

As far as his general statement is concerned, your son is correct: not everyone who can afford it needs or should be given a college education. Some people by natural or acquired disposition find no interests in academic subjects and simply would be wasting their time in pursuing higher education. Once that disposition has been discovered to be rather immutably formed, the person should be allowed to follow his interests since by doing so he will find satisfaction in his work (which consumes a great part of living) and probably be a more productive member of the community.

Since college age people are frequently close to an immutable disposition, I would suggest that parents in a case like yours think in terms of compromise. For example, they could promise to help the youngster with his aspirations provided that he finishes college or at least stays with it for another year or two.

Index